1 Table of contents

Abstract

This book is designed to provide practical solutions to real-world applications using JavaScript. It presents hands-on projects, guiding readers from basic Document Object Model (DOM) usage to more advanced Object-Oriented Programming (OOP) applications. Whether you are a beginner or an intermediate developer, this book will help you strengthen your JavaScript skills by building practical, functional applications. With clear explanations, hands-on exercises, and a progressive structure, this book serves as an invaluable resource for anyone looking to master JavaScript programming.

The book is divided into four chapters:

Chapter 1: Document Object Model

Applications: Dynamic Form Creation, Real Time Clock, Form Validation, Slideshow Functionality, Content loading, Drag elements, Search Functionality, Simple Calculator, Smooth Scrolling, Drop down Menu, Data table creation, Quiz application.

Chapter 2: Student Management System using JavaScript

Chapter 3: jQuery

Applications: Todo List, Real-Time search filter, Pagination system, Sortable table columns, Form validation, Navbar, Authentication page, Ajax (Get request), Ajax (Post request), Ajax Data visualization, Carousel slider

Chapter 4: Practical Applications with Object-Oriented Programming

Applications: Blog post management, User authentication system, Shopping cart (with local storage), Messaging system (with local storage)

Introduction

JavaScript is one of the most widely used programming languages in the world, driving the dynamic and interactive features of modern web applications. Whether you're new to programming or looking to deepen your understanding, this book is designed to guide you through practical exercises that will enable you to build powerful and functional web applications.

The chapters in this book cover fundamental concepts and progressively advance to more complex topics. In Chapter 1, you'll explore how to manipulate the Document Object Model (DOM) to create interactive applications. Chapter 2 focuses on building a complete student management system using JavaScript. In Chapter 3, you will learn to implement practical applications using jQuery, a popular JavaScript library that simplifies DOM manipulation. Finally, Chapter 4 delves into Object-Oriented Programming (OOP) in JavaScript, where you'll build advanced applications using OOP principles.

Chapter 1
Document Object Model

1 Document Object Model

1.1 Exercises

1.1.1 Introduction to DOM

Exercise 1.1.1 Change Text Content

1. Find the paragraph element by its ID (`targetPara`).

2. Change its text content to "Hello world" when a button is clicked (Example: Figure 1.1.1).

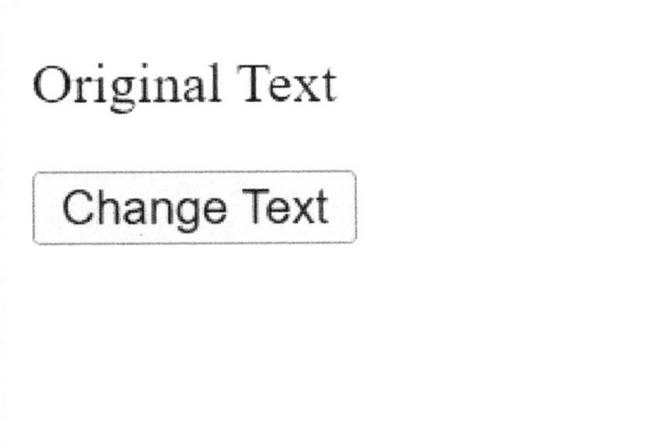

Original Text

Change Text

Figure 1.1.1 Change text

Basic Html File:

```
<!DOCTYPE html>
<html lang="en">
<head>
    <meta charset="UTF-8">
    <title>Exercise 1.1.1</title>
</head>
<body>
    <p id="targetPara">Original Text</p>
    <button id="changeTextButton">Change Text</button>
</body>
</html>
```

Exercise 1.1.2 Change Styling

1. Find the div element by its ID (`boxDiv`).

2. Change its background color to "blue" when a button is clicked (Example: Figure 1.1.2).

Figure 1.1.2 Change Styling

Basic Html File:

```
<!DOCTYPE html>
<html lang="en">
<head>
    <meta charset="UTF-8">
    <title>Exercise 1.1.2</title>
    <style>
        #boxDiv {
            width: 200px;
            height: 200px;
            background-color: #f0f0f0;
        }
```

```
    </style>
</head>
<body>
    <div id="boxDiv">This is a box</div>
    <button id="changeColorButton">Change Color</button>
</body>
</html>
```

Exercise 1.1.3 Add New Element

1. Find the unordered list element by its ID (`list`).

2. Append a new list item with the text "Madrid" when a button is clicked (Example: Figure 1.1.3).

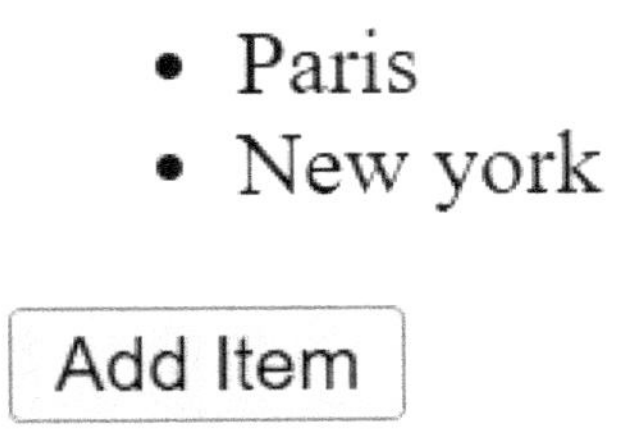

- Paris
- New york

Add Item

Figure 1.1.3 Add new list element

Basic Html File:

```
<!DOCTYPE html>
<html lang="en">
<head>
    <meta charset="UTF-8">
    <title>Exercise 1.1.3</title>
</head>
<body>
    <ul id="list">
        <li>Paris</li>
        <li>New york</li>
```

```
    </ul>
    <button id="addItemButton">Add Item</button>
</body>
</html>
```

Exercise 1.1.4 Remove Element

1. Find the div element by its ID (`containerDiv`).

2. Remove its first paragraph child element when a button is clicked (Example: Figure 1.1.4).

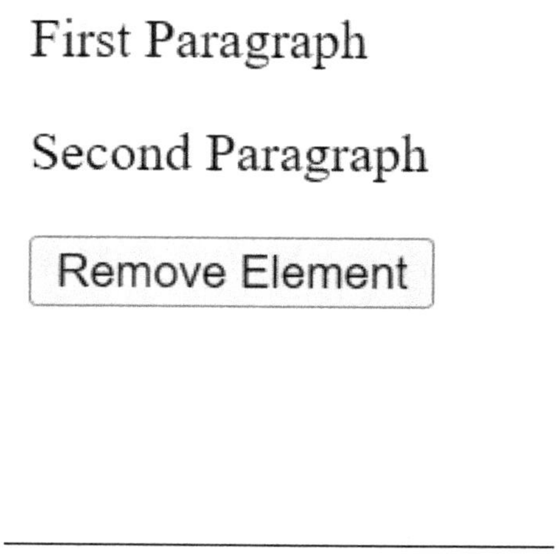

First Paragraph

Second Paragraph

Remove Element

Figure 1.1.4 Remove element

Basic Html File:

```
<!DOCTYPE html>
<html lang="en">
<head>
    <meta charset="UTF-8">
    <title>Exercise 1.1.4</title>
</head>
<body>
    <div id="containerDiv">
        <p> First Paragraph </p>
        <p>Second Paragraph </p>
    </div>
    <button id="removeElementButton">Remove Element</button>
```

```
</body>
</html>
```

Exercise 1.1.5 Update Text Content with Input Value

1. Find the input element by its ID (`textInput`).

2. Find the paragraph element by its ID (`targetPara`).

3. Update the paragraph's text content with the value entered in the input field when a button is clicked (Example: Figure 1.1.5).

Enter text | Update Text |

Hello

Figure 1.1.5 Update text content

Basic Html File:

```
<!DOCTYPE html>
<html lang="en">
<head>
    <meta charset="UTF-8">
    <title>Exercise 1.1.5</title>
</head>
<body>
    <input type="text" id="textInput" placeholder="Enter text">
    <button id="updateTextButton">Update Text</button>
    <p id="targetPara"> Hello </p>
</body>
</html>
```

Exercise 1.1.6 Toggle Class on Click

1. Find the paragraph element by its ID (`targetPara`).

2. Toggle a CSS class named "highlight" on the paragraph when it is clicked (Example: Figure 1.1.6).

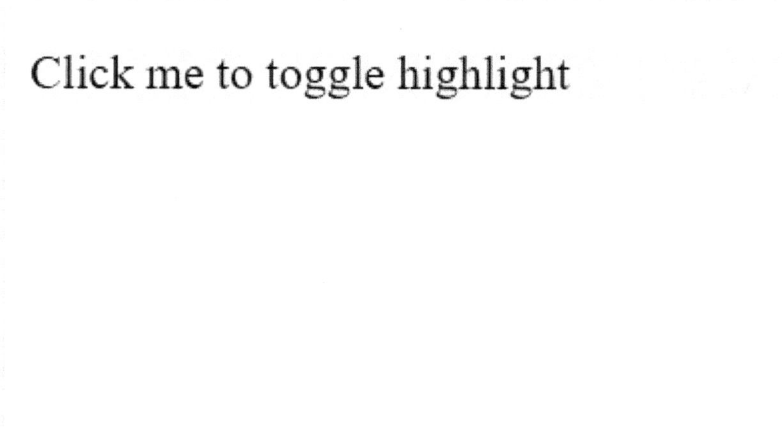

Click me to toggle highlight

Figure 1.1.6 Toggle class on click

Basic Html File:

```
<!DOCTYPE html>
<html lang="en">
<head>
    <meta charset="UTF-8">
    <title>Exercise 1.1.6</title>
    <style>
        .highlight {
            background-color: yellow;
        }
    </style>
</head>
<body>
    <p id="targetPara">Click me to toggle highlight</p>
</body>
</html>
```

Exercise 1.1.7 Add and Remove List Items

1. Find the unordered list element by its ID (`list`).

2. Add a new list item with the text "New Item" when a button is clicked.

3. Remove the last list item when another button is clicked (Example: Figure 1.1.7).

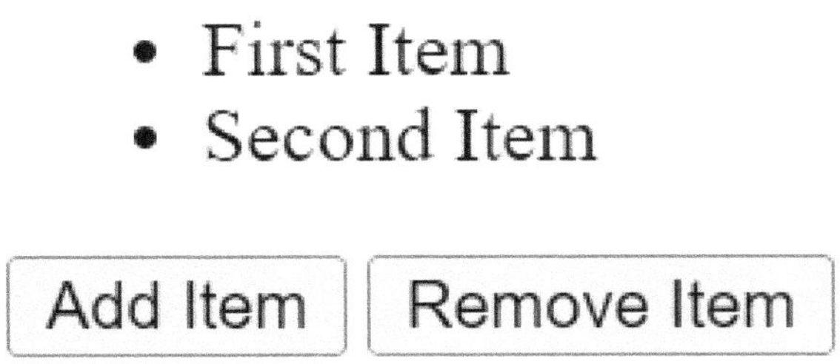

- First Item
- Second Item

[Add Item] [Remove Item]

Figure 1.1.7 Add\Remove item

Basic Html File:

```html
<!DOCTYPE html>
<html lang="en">
<head>
    <meta charset="UTF-8">
    <title>Exercise 1.1.7</title>
</head>
<body>
    <ul id="list">
        <li>First Item </li>
        <li>Second Item </li>
    </ul>
    <button id="addItemButton">Add Item</button>
    <button id="removeItemButton">Remove Item</button>
    </body>
</html>
```

Exercise 1.1.8 Show and Hide Element

1. Find the div element by its ID (`contentDiv`).

2. Toggle its visibility when a button is clicked (Example: Figure 1.1.8)

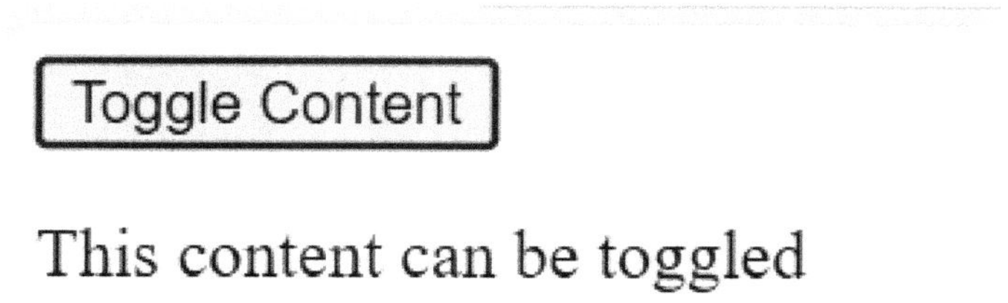

Toggle Content

This content can be toggled

Figure 1.1.8 Show and hide element

Basic Html File:

```
<!DOCTYPE html>
<html lang="en">
<head>
    <meta charset="UTF-8">
    <title>Exercise 1.1.8</title>
    <style>
        #contentDiv {
            display: none;
        }
    </style>
</head>
<body>
    <button id="toggleButton">Toggle Content</button>
    <div id="contentDiv">
        <p>This content can be toggled</p>
    </div>
</body>
</html>
```

Exercise 1.1.9: Event Delegation

1. Create a list with multiple list items.

2. Dynamically add event listeners to each list item so that clicking on any list item log its text content to the console.

Basic Html File:

```
<!DOCTYPE html>
<html lang="en">
<head>
    <meta charset="UTF-8">
    <title>Exercise 1.1.9</title>
</head>
<body>
    <ul id="list">
        <li>Paris</li>
        <li>Madrid</li>
        <li>New york</li>
    </ul>
</body>
</html>
```

Exercise 1.1.10: Create and Append Elements

Create new elements and append them to the DOM dynamically.

1. Create a button.

2. Create a new paragraph element with the text "Hello world".

3. Append the paragraph to the body when the button is clicked (Example: Figure 1.1.10).

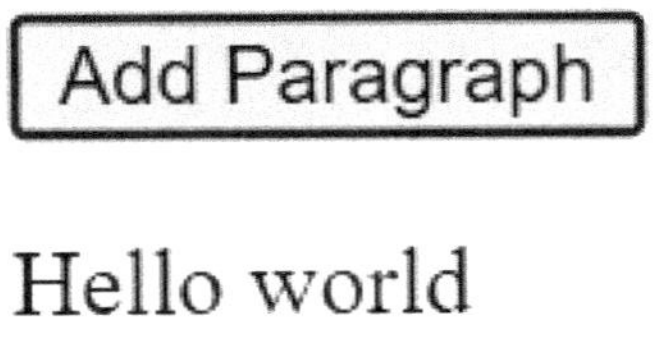

Add Paragraph

Hello world

Figure 1.1.10 Create and append element

Basic Html File:

```
<!DOCTYPE html>
<html lang="en">
<head>
    <meta charset="UTF-8">
```

```
    <title>Exercise 1.1.10</title>
</head>
<body>
    <button id="addParagraphButton">Add Paragraph</button>
</body>
</html>
```

1.1.2 DOM manipulation

Exercise 1.2.1 Dynamic Form Creation

Write a function that dynamically generates a form with input fields for name, address, and email, and appends it to a specific div in the document (Example: Figure 1.2.1).

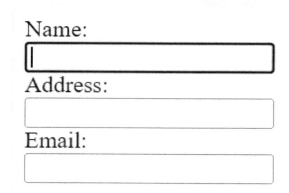

Figure 1.2.1 Form creation

Basic Html File:

```
<!DOCTYPE html>
<html lang="en">
<head>
    <meta charset="UTF-8">
    <title>Exercise 1.2.1: Dynamic Form Creation</title>
</head>
```

```
<body>
<div id="dynamicFormDiv">
    <!-- The dynamically generated form will be appended here -->
</div>
</body>
</html>
```

Exercise 1.2.2 Real-Time Clock

Implement a program that retrieves the current date and time, and displays it in a specific paragraph element in real-time (Example: Figure 1.2.2).

07/10/2024 12:34:25

Figure 1.2.2 Real time Clock

Basic Html File:

```
<!DOCTYPE html>
<html lang="en">
<head>
    <meta charset="UTF-8">
    <title>Exercise 1.2.2: Real-Time Clock</title>
</head>
<body>
<p id="clock">
    <!-- The real-time clock will be displayed here -->
</p>
</body>
</html>
```

Exercise 1.2.3 Form Validation

Write a function that validates a form before submission, checking if all required fields are filled and displaying error messages if necessary (Example: Figure 1.2.3).

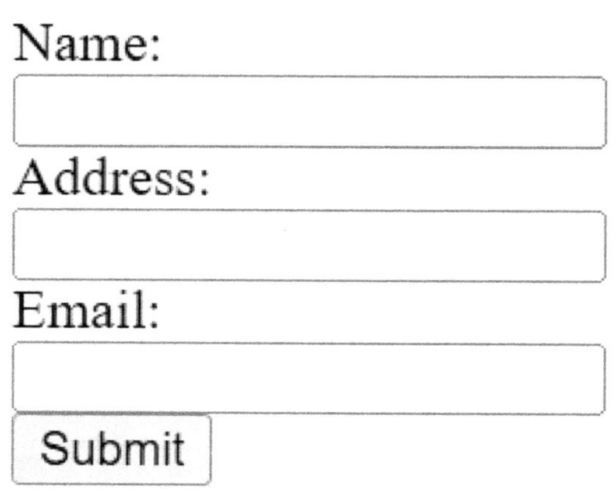

Name:

Address:

Email:

Submit

Figure 1.2.3 Form validation

Basic Html File:

```html
<!DOCTYPE html>
<html lang="en">
<head>
    <meta charset="UTF-8">
    <title>Exercise 1.2.3: Form Validation</title>
</head>
<body>
<form id="validationForm">
    <label for="name">Name:</label><br>
    <input type="text" id="name" name="name"><br>
    <label for="address">Address:</label><br>
    <input type="text" id="address" name="address"><br>
    <label for="email">Email:</label><br>
    <input type="email" id="email" name="email"><br>
    <button type="submit">Submit</button>
    <div id="error" style="color: red;"></div>
</form>
</body>
</html>
```

Exercise 1.2.4 Slideshow Functionality

Create a slideshow functionality using JavaScript, where images cycle through in a specific container div with next and previous buttons for navigation (Example: Figure 1.2.4).

Figure 1.2.4 Slideshow Functionality

Basic Html File:

```
<!DOCTYPE html>
<html lang="en">
<head>
    <meta charset="UTF-8">
    <title>Exercise 1.2.4: Slideshow Functionality</title>
    <style>
        /* Style for slideshow container */
        #slideshow {
            width: 600px;
            height: 400px;
            margin: 0 auto;
            overflow: hidden;
            position: relative;
```

```css
    border: 1px solid #ccc;
}
 /* Style for images */
.slide {
    display: none;
    width: 100%;
    height: 100%;
    position: absolute;
    top: 0;
    left: 0;
}


/* Style for navigation buttons */
.prev, .next {
    cursor: pointer;
    position: absolute;
    top: 50%;
    transform: translateY(-50%);
    background-color: rgba(0, 0, 0, 0.5);
    color: white;
    font-size: 24px;
    padding: 10px;
    border: none;
    z-index: 100;
}
.prev {
    left: 0;
}
.next {
    right: 0;
}
```
```html
    </style>
</head>
<body>
<div id="slideshow">
    <!-- Example images -->
```

```html
    <img class="slide" src="example1.jpg" alt="Image 1">
    <img class="slide" src="example2.jpg" alt="Image 2">
    <img class="slide" src="example3.jpg" alt="Image 3">
    <!-- Navigation buttons -->
    <button class="prev" onclick="prevSlide()">&#10094;</button>
    <button class="next" onclick="nextSlide()">&#10095;</button>
</div>
</body>
</html>
```

Exercise 1.2.5 Content Loading

Write a program that allows users to fetch data from an array of objects and display it in a specific section of the document (Example: Figure 1.2.5).

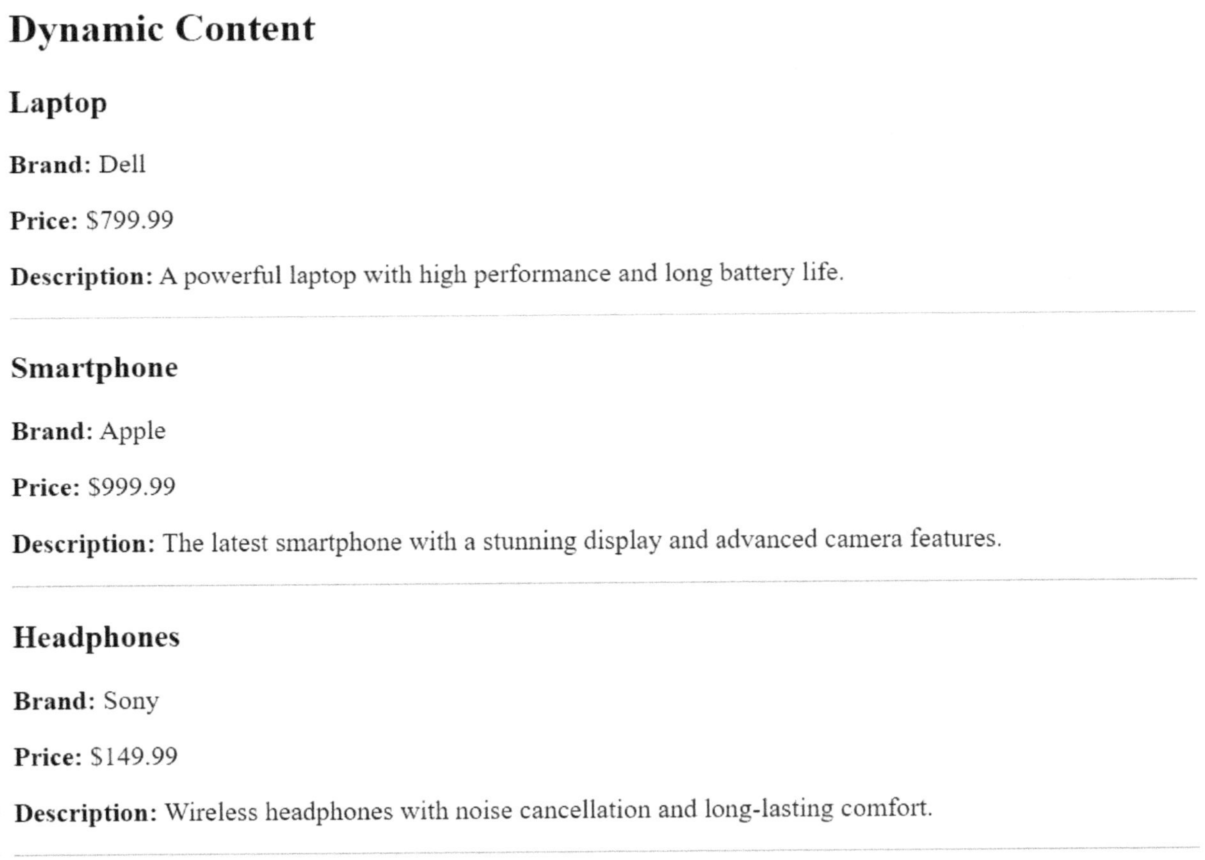

Dynamic Content

Laptop

Brand: Dell

Price: $799.99

Description: A powerful laptop with high performance and long battery life.

Smartphone

Brand: Apple

Price: $999.99

Description: The latest smartphone with a stunning display and advanced camera features.

Headphones

Brand: Sony

Price: $149.99

Description: Wireless headphones with noise cancellation and long-lasting comfort.

Figure 1.2.5 Content loading

Basic Html File:

```html
<!DOCTYPE html>
<html lang="en">
<head>
    <meta charset="UTF-8">
    <title>Exercise 1.2.5:  Content Loading</title>
</head>
<body>
<div id="contentSection">
    <h2>Content</h2>
    <!-- Data will be displayed dynamically here -->
</div>
<script>
        const products = [
            {
                id: 1,
                name: 'Laptop',
                brand: 'Dell',
                price: 799.99,
                description: 'A powerful laptop with high performance
and long battery life.'
            },
            {
                id: 2,
                name: 'Smartphone',
                brand: 'Apple',
                price: 999.99,
                description: 'The latest smartphone with a stunning
display and advanced camera features.'
            },
            {
                id: 3,
                name: 'Headphones',
                brand: 'Sony',
                price: 149.99,
```

```
        description: 'Wireless headphones with noise
cancellation and long-lasting comfort.'
        }
    ];
</script>
</body>
</html>
```

Exercise 1.2.6 Drag elements

Implement a feature that allows users to drag elements within a specific container div using mouse events (Example: Figure 1.2.6).

Figure 1.2.6 Drag elements

Basic Html File:

```
<!DOCTYPE html>
<html lang="en">
<head>
    <meta charset="UTF-8">
    <title>Exercise 1.2.6</title>
    <style>
        /* CSS styles for drag-and-drop */
        #container {
            width: 400px;
```

```
            height: 300px;
            border: 2px solid #ccc;
            padding: 10px;
            margin: 50px auto;
            position: relative;
        }


        .draggable {
            width: 100px;
            height: 50px;
            background-color: #f0f0f0;
            border: 1px solid #999;
            border-radius: 5px;
            padding: 10px;
            cursor: pointer;
            position: absolute;
        }
    </style>
</head>
<body>
    <div id="container">
        <div class="draggable" style="top: 50px; left: 50px;">Drag
me</div>
        <div class="draggable" style="top: 120px; left: 120px;">Drag
me too</div>
        <!-- Add more draggable elements here -->
    </div>
</body>
</html>
```

Exercise 1.2.7 Search Functionality

Develop a search functionality that filters a list of items dynamically as users type into an input field, displaying matching results instantly (Example: Figure 1.2.7).

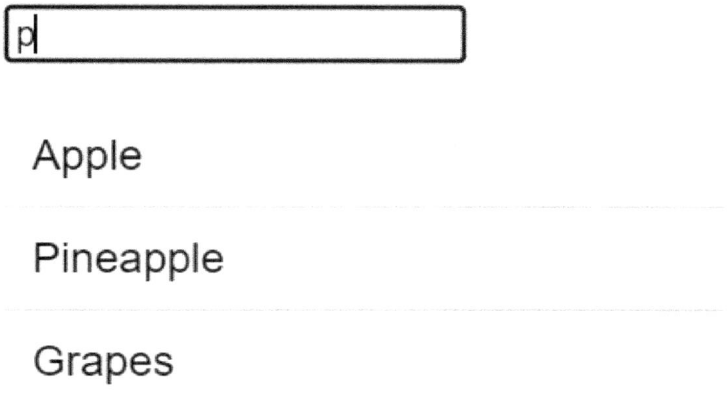

p|

Apple

Pineapple

Grapes

Figure 1.2.7: Search Functionality

Basic Html File:

```
<!DOCTYPE html>
<html lang="en">
<head>
  <meta charset="UTF-8">
    <title>Exercise 1.2.7</title>
  <style>
    body {
      font-family: Arial, sans-serif;
    }
    ul {
      list-style-type: none;
      padding: 0;
    }
    li {
      padding: 10px;
      border-bottom: 1px solid #ccc;
    }
    li:last-child {
      border-bottom: none;
    }
  </style>
</head>
```

```
<body>
    <input type="text" id="searchInput" placeholder="Search...">
    <ul id="resultsList"></ul>
    <script>
        // Sample list of items (can be fetched dynamically from a
server)
        var items = [
            'Apple',
            'Banana',
            'Orange',
            'Mango',
            'Pineapple',
            'Grapes',
            'Watermelon',
            'Kiwi',
            'Strawberry',
            'Blueberry'
        ];
    </script>
</body>
</html>
```

Exercise 1.2.8 simple calculator

Create a simple calculator application using JavaScript that can perform basic arithmetic operations like addition, subtraction, multiplication, and division (Example: Figure 1.2.8).

Simple Calculator

Enter first number:

```
3
```

Enter second number:

```
5
```

Choose an operation:

```
Addition          ⌄     Calculate
```

Result: 8

Figure 1.2.8 simple calculator

Basic Html File:

```html
<!DOCTYPE html>
<html lang="en">
<head>
    <meta charset="UTF-8">
    <title>Exercise 1.2.8: Simple Calculator</title>
    <style>
        label {
            display: block;
            margin-bottom: 5px;
        }
        input[type="number"] {
            width: 200px;
            margin-bottom: 10px;
        }
        select {
            width: 200px;
```

```
            margin-bottom: 10px;
        }
        button {
            padding: 8px 16px;
            background-color: #4CAF50;
            color: white;
            border: none;
            border-radius: 4px;
            cursor: pointer;
        }
        button:hover {
            background-color: #45a049;
        }
    </style>
</head>
<body>
    <h2>Simple Calculator</h2>
    <label for="num1">Enter first number:</label>
    <input type="number" id="num1">
    <label for="num2">Enter second number:</label>
    <input type="number" id="num2">
    <label for="operation">Choose an operation:</label>
    <select id="operation">
        <option value="+">Addition</option>
        <option value="-">Subtraction</option>
        <option value="*">Multiplication</option>
        <option value="/">Division</option>
    </select>
    <button onclick="calculate()">Calculate</button>
    <p id="result"></p>
</body>
</html>
```

Exercise 1.2.9 Smooth Scrolling

Implement a feature that automatically scrolls to a specific section of the page when a link within the document is clicked.

Basic Html File:

```html
<!DOCTYPE html>
<html lang="en">
<head>
  <meta charset="UTF-8">
    <title>Exercise 1.2.9</title>
  <style>
    /* Styles for demonstration purpose only */
    body {
      font-family: Arial, sans-serif;
      margin: 0;
      padding: 0;
    }
    header {
      background-color: #333;
      color: #fff;
      padding: 10px;
      text-align: center;
    }
    nav {
      display: flex;
      justify-content: center;
      margin-bottom: 20px;
    }
    nav a {
      text-decoration: none;
      margin: 0 10px;
    }
    section {
      padding: 20px;
      margin: 20px 0;
      border: 1px solid #ccc;
    }
  </style>
</head>
```

```
<body>
<header>
  <h1>Scroll to Section</h1>
</header>
<nav>
  <a href="#section1">Product Description</a>
  <a href="#section2">Customer Reviews</a>
  <a href="#section3">Related Products</a>
</nav>
<section id="section1">
  <h2>Product Description</h2>
  <p>This section provides detailed information about our featured
product..</p>
</section>
<section id="section2">
  <h2>Customer Reviews</h2>
  <p>Here you can find reviews from our customers who have purchased
this product. </p>
</section>
<section id="section3">
  <h2>Related Products</h2>
<p>Here,you can find similar products</p>
</section>
</body>
</html>
```

Exercise 1.2.10 Dropdown Menu:

Create a dropdown menu functionality using JavaScript that expands and collapses when clicked, revealing hidden options (Example: Figure 1.2.10).

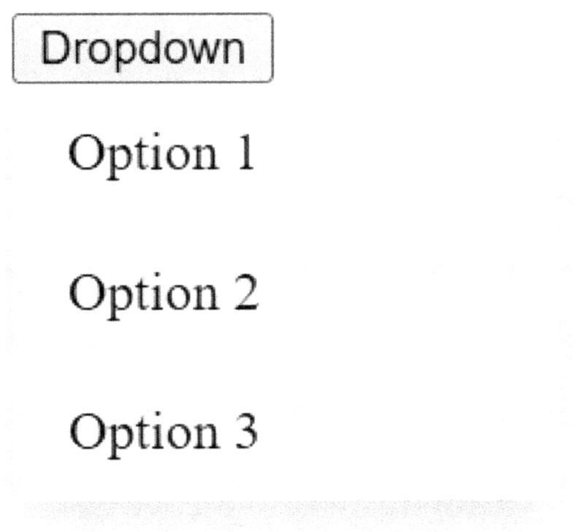

Dropdown

Option 1

Option 2

Option 3

Figure 1.2.10 Dropdown Menu

Basic Html File:

```html
<!DOCTYPE html>
<html lang="en">
<head>
    <meta charset="UTF-8">
    <title>Exercise 1.2.10</title>
    <style>
        /* Styles for the dropdown menu */
        .dropdown {
            position: relative;
            display: inline-block;
        }
        .dropdown-content {
            display: none;
            position: absolute;
            background-color: #f9f9f9;
            min-width: 160px;
            box-shadow: 0px 8px 16px 0px rgba(0,0,0,0.2);
            z-index: 1;
        }
        .dropdown-content a {
```

```
                color: black;

                padding: 12px 16px;

                text-decoration: none;

                display: block;

            }

        .dropdown-content a:hover {

                background-color: #f1f1f1;

            }

        .dropdown:hover .dropdown-content {

                display: block;

            }

    </style>

</head>

<body>

<div class="dropdown">

    <button class="dropbtn">Dropdown</button>

    <div class="dropdown-content">

        <a href="#">Option 1</a>

        <a href="#">Option 2</a>

        <a href="#">Option 3</a>

    </div>

</div>

</section>

</body>

</html>
```

Exercise 1.2.11 Data Table Creation:

Write a program that generates a table with data retrieved from an array of objects and displays it in a specific section of the document (Example: Figure 1.2.11).

Dynamic Table

name	age	city
John Doe	30	New York
Jane Smith	25	Los Angeles
Michael Johnson	35	Chicago

Figure 1.2.11 Table creation

Basic Html File:

```html
<!DOCTYPE html>
<html lang="en">
<head>
    <meta charset="UTF-8">
    <title>Exercise 1.2.11: Dynamic Table</title>
    <style>
        /* CSS for table borders */
        table {
            border-collapse: collapse;
            width: 100%;
        }
        th, td {
            border: 1px solid #dddddd;
            text-align: left;
            padding: 8px;
        }
        th {
            background-color: #f2f2f2;
        }
    </style>
</head>
<body>
```

```
<h2>Dynamic Table</h2>
<div id="tableContainer"></div>
<script>
    // Sample array of objects with real data
    const data = [
        { name: "John Doe", age: 30, city: "New York" },
        { name: "Jane Smith", age: 25, city: "Los Angeles" },
        { name: "Michael Johnson", age: 35, city: "Chicago" }
    ];
</script>
</body>
</html>
```

Exercise 1.2.12 Quiz Application :

Create a quiz application using JavaScript where users can answer multiple-choice questions and receive feedback on their answers dynamically (Example: Figure 1.2.12).

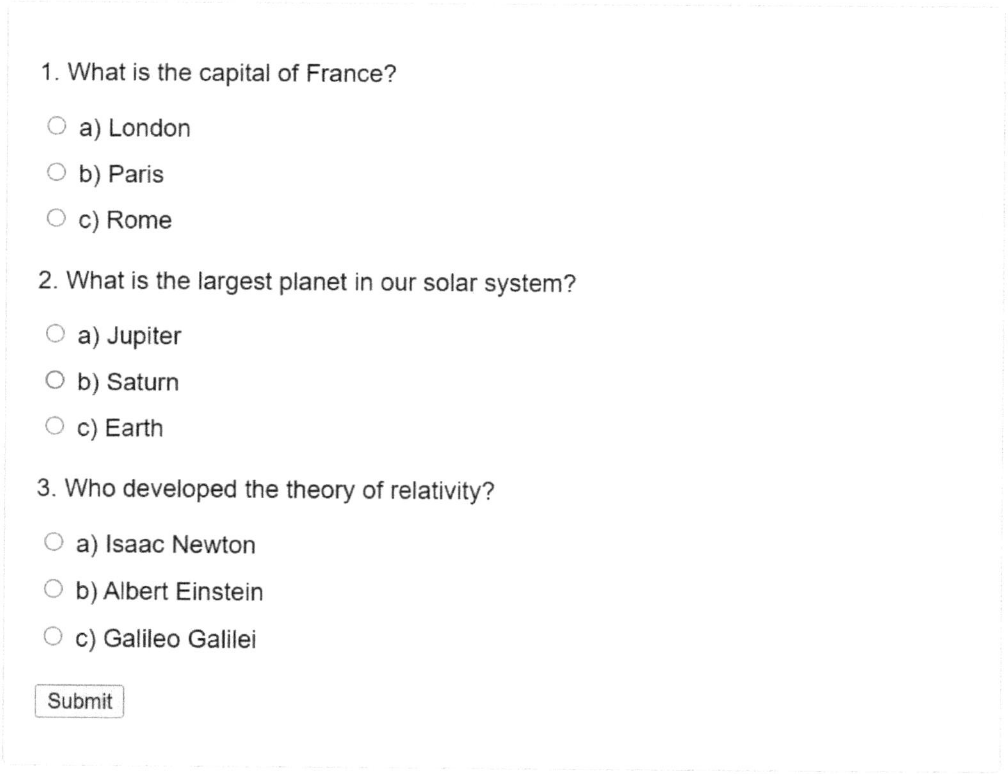

1. What is the capital of France?

○ a) London

○ b) Paris

○ c) Rome

2. What is the largest planet in our solar system?

○ a) Jupiter

○ b) Saturn

○ c) Earth

3. Who developed the theory of relativity?

○ a) Isaac Newton

○ b) Albert Einstein

○ c) Galileo Galilei

Submit

Figure 1.2.12 Quiz Application

Basic Html File:

```html
<!DOCTYPE html>
<html lang="en">
<head>
    <meta charset="UTF-8">
    <title>Exercise 1.2.12: Quiz Application</title>
    <style>
        /* CSS styles */
        body {
            font-family: Arial, sans-serif;
        }
        .quiz-container {
            max-width: 600px;
            margin: 0 auto;
            padding: 20px;
            border: 1px solid #ccc;
            border-radius: 5px;
        }
        .question {
            margin-bottom: 20px;
        }
        .options label {
            display: block;
            margin-bottom: 10px;
        }
        .feedback {
            font-weight: bold;
            margin-top: 10px;
        }
    </style>
</head>
<body>
    <div class="quiz-container">
        <div class="question">
            <p>1. What is the capital of France?</p>
```

```html
        <div class="options">
            <label><input type="radio" name="q1" value="a"> a)
London</label>
            <label><input type="radio" name="q1" value="b"> b)
Paris</label>
            <label><input type="radio" name="q1" value="c"> c)
Rome</label>
        </div>
    </div>
    <div class="question">
        <p>2. What is the largest planet in our solar
system?</p>
        <div class="options">
            <label><input type="radio" name="q2" value="a"> a)
Jupiter</label>
            <label><input type="radio" name="q2" value="b"> b)
Saturn</label>
            <label><input type="radio" name="q2" value="c"> c)
Earth</label>
        </div>
    </div>
    <div class="question">
        <p>3. Who developed the theory of relativity?</p>
        <div class="options">
            <label><input type="radio" name="q3" value="a"> a)
Isaac Newton</label>
            <label><input type="radio" name="q3" value="b"> b)
Albert Einstein</label>
            <label><input type="radio" name="q3" value="c"> c)
Galileo Galilei</label>
        </div>
    </div>
    <button onclick="submitQuiz()">Submit</button>
    <div id="quizFeedback" class="feedback"></div>
    </div>
</body>
```

```html
</html>
```

1.2 Solutions

1.2.1 Introduction to DOM

Exercise 1.1.1: Change Text Content

Html File:

```html
<!DOCTYPE html>
<html lang="en">
<head>
  <meta charset="UTF-8">
  <title>Exercise 1.1.1</title>
</head>
<body>
  <p id="targetPara">Original Text</p>
  <button id="changeTextButton">Change Text</button>
  <script>
    // Find the paragraph element and button by their IDs.
    var para = document.getElementById("targetPara");
    var button = document.getElementById("changeTextButton");
    // Add event listener to the button.
    button.addEventListener("click", function () {
      // Change the text content of the paragraph.
      para.textContent = "Hello world";
    });
  </script>
</body>
</html>
```

Exercise 1.1.2: Change Styling

Html File:

```html
<!DOCTYPE html>
<html lang="en">
<head>
```

```html
    <meta charset="UTF-8">
    <title>Exercise 1.1.2</title>
    <style>
        #boxDiv {
            width: 200px;
            height: 200px;
            background-color: #f0f0f0;
        }
    </style>
</head>
<body>
    <div id="boxDiv">This is a box</div>
    <button id="changeColorButton">Change Color</button>
    <script>
        // Find the div element and button by their IDs.
        var div = document.getElementById("boxDiv");
        var button = document.getElementById("changeColorButton");
        // Add event listener to the button.
        button.addEventListener("click", function () {
            // Change the background color of the div.
            div.style.backgroundColor = "blue";
        });
    </script>
</body>
</html>
```

Exercise 1.1.3: Add New Element

Html File:

```html
<!DOCTYPE html>
<html lang="en">
<head>
    <meta charset="UTF-8">
    <title>Exercise 1.1.3</title>
```

```
</head>
<body>
  <ul id="list">
    <li>Paris</li>
    <li>New york</li>
  </ul>
  <button id="addItemButton">Add Item</button>
  <script>
    // Find the unordered list element and button by their IDs.
    var list = document.getElementById("list");
    var button = document.getElementById("addItemButton");
    // Add event listener to the button.
    button.addEventListener("click", function () {
      // Create a new list item.
      var newItem = document.createElement("li");
      newItem.textContent = "Madrid";
      // Append the new item to the list.
      list.appendChild(newItem);
    });
  </script>
</body>
</html>
```

Exercise 1.1.4: Remove Element

Html File:

```
<!DOCTYPE html>
<html lang="en">
<head>
  <meta charset="UTF-8">
  <title>Exercise 1.1.4</title>
</head>
<body>
  <div id="containerDiv">
```

```
    <p> First Paragraph </p>
    <p>Second Paragraph </p>
  </div>
  <button id="removeElementButton">Remove Element</button>
  <script>
    // Find the container div element and button by their IDs.
    var container = document.getElementById("containerDiv");
    var button = document.getElementById("removeElementButton");
    // Add event listener to the button.
    button.addEventListener("click", function () {
      // Remove the first paragraph child element.
      container.removeChild(container.firstElementChild);
    });
  </script>
</body>
</html>
```

Exercise 1.1.5: Update Text Content with Input Value

Html File:

```
<!DOCTYPE html>
<html lang="en">
<head>
  <meta charset="UTF-8">
  <title>Exercise 1.1.5</title>
</head>
<body>
  <input type="text" id="textInput" placeholder="Enter text">
  <button id="updateTextButton">Update Text</button>
  <p id="targetPara"> Hello </p>
  <script>
    // Find the input element, paragraph element, and button by their IDs.
    var input = document.getElementById("textInput");
    var para = document.getElementById("targetPara");
```

```
    var button = document.getElementById("updateTextButton");
    // Add event listener to the button.
    button.addEventListener("click", function () {
        // Update the paragraph's text content with the input value.
        para.textContent = input.value;
    });
    </script>
</body>
</html>
```

Exercise 1.1.6: Toggle Class on Click

Html File:

```
<!DOCTYPE html>
<html lang="en">
<head>
    <meta charset="UTF-8">
    <title>Exercise 1.1.6</title>
    <style>
        .highlight {
            background-color: yellow;
        }
    </style>
</head>
<body>
    <p id="targetPara">Click me to toggle highlight</p>
    <script>
        // Find the paragraph element by its ID.
        var para = document.getElementById("targetPara");
        // Add event listener to the paragraph.
        para.addEventListener("click", function () {
            // Toggle the "highlight" class on the paragraph.
            para.classList.toggle("highlight");
        });
```

```html
  </script>
</body>
</html>
```

Exercise 1.1.7: Add and Remove List Items

Html File:

```html
<!DOCTYPE html>
<html lang="en">
<head>
  <meta charset="UTF-8">
  <title>Exercise 1.1.7</title>
</head>
<body>
  <ul id="list">
    <li>First Item </li>
    <li>Second Item </li>
  </ul>
  <button id="addItemButton">Add Item</button>
  <button id="removeItemButton">Remove Item</button>
  <script>
    // Find the unordered list element and buttons by their IDs.
    var list = document.getElementById("list");
    var addItemButton = document.getElementById("addItemButton");
    var removeItemButton = document.getElementById("removeItemButton");
    // Add event listener to the "Add Item" button.
    addItemButton.addEventListener("click", function () {
      // Create a new list item.
      var newItem = document.createElement("li");
      newItem.textContent = "New Item";
      // Append the new item to the list.
      list.appendChild(newItem);
    });
    // Add event listener to the "Remove Item" button.
```

```
        removeItemButton.addEventListener("click", function () {
            // Remove the last list item.
            var lastItem = list.lastElementChild;
            if (lastItem) {
                list.removeChild(lastItem);
            }
        });
    </script>
</body>
</html>
```

Exercise 1.1.8: Show and Hide Element

Html File:

```
<!DOCTYPE html>
<html lang="en">
<head>
    <meta charset="UTF-8">
    <title>Exercise 1.1.8</title>
    <style>
        #contentDiv {
            display: none;
        }
    </style>
</head>
<body>
    <button id="toggleButton">Toggle Content</button>
    <div id="contentDiv">
        <p>This content can be toggled</p>
    </div>
    <script>
        // Find the div element and button by their IDs.
        var contentDiv = document.getElementById("contentDiv");
        var toggleButton = document.getElementById("toggleButton");
```

```
    // Add event listener to the button.
    toggleButton.addEventListener("click", function () {
        // Toggle the visibility of the content div.
        if (contentDiv.style.display === "none") {
            contentDiv.style.display = "block";
        } else {
            contentDiv.style.display = "none";
        }
    });
    </script>
</body>
</html>
```

Exercise 1.1.9: Event Delegation

Html File:

```
<!DOCTYPE html>
<html lang="en">
<head>
    <meta charset="UTF-8">
    <title>Exercise 1.1.9</title>
</head>
<body>
    <ul id="list">
        <li>Paris</li>
        <li>Madrid</li>
        <li>New york</li>
    </ul>
    <script>
        // Find the unordered list element by its ID.
        var list = document.getElementById("list");
        // Add event listener to the list.
        list.addEventListener("click", function (event) {
            // Check if the clicked target is an <li> element.
```

```
            if (event.target.tagName === "LI") {
                // Log the text content of the clicked <li> element.
                console.log(event.target.textContent);
            }
        });
    </script>
</body>
</html>
```

Exercise 1.1.10: Create and Append Elements

Html File:

```
<!DOCTYPE html>
<html lang="en">
<head>
    <meta charset="UTF-8">
    <title>Exercise 1.1.10</title>
</head>
<body>
    <button id="addParagraphButton">Add Paragraph</button>
    <script>
        // Find the button element by its ID.
        var addButton = document.getElementById("addParagraphButton");
        // Add event listener to the button.
        addButton.addEventListener("click", function () {
            // Create a new paragraph element.
            var newParagraph = document.createElement("p");
            newParagraph.textContent = "Hello world";
            // Append the paragraph to the body.
            document.body.appendChild(newParagraph);
        });
    </script>
</body>
</html>
```

1.2.2 DOM manipulation

Exercise 1.2.1 Dynamic Form Creation:

Html File (dynamic_form.html):

```html
<!DOCTYPE html>
<html lang="en">
<head>
  <meta charset="UTF-8">
  <title>Exercise 1.2.1</title>
</head>
<body>
  <div id="dynamicFormDiv">
    <!-- The dynamically generated form will be appended here -->
  </div>
  <script src="dynamic_form.js"></script>
</body>
</html>
```

JavaScript File(dynamic_form.js):

```javascript
// Function to create the dynamic form
function createForm() {
    // Get the div where the form will be appended
    const formDiv = document.getElementById('dynamicFormDiv');

    // Create form element
    const form = document.createElement('form');

    // Create input fields for Name, Address, and Email
    const nameLabel = document.createElement('label');
    nameLabel.textContent = 'Name:';
    const nameInput = document.createElement('input');
    nameInput.setAttribute('type', 'text');
    nameInput.setAttribute('name', 'name');
```

```javascript
const addressLabel = document.createElement('label');
addressLabel.textContent = 'Address:';
const addressInput = document.createElement('input');
addressInput.setAttribute('type', 'text');
addressInput.setAttribute('name', 'address');

const emailLabel = document.createElement('label');
emailLabel.textContent = 'Email:';
const emailInput = document.createElement('input');
emailInput.setAttribute('type', 'email');
emailInput.setAttribute('name', 'email');

// Append labels and inputs to the form
form.appendChild(nameLabel);
form.appendChild(document.createElement('br'));
form.appendChild(nameInput);
form.appendChild(document.createElement('br'));
form.appendChild(addressLabel);
form.appendChild(document.createElement('br'));
form.appendChild(addressInput);
form.appendChild(document.createElement('br'));
form.appendChild(emailLabel);
form.appendChild(document.createElement('br'));
form.appendChild(emailInput);
form.appendChild(document.createElement('br'));

// Append form to the div
formDiv.appendChild(form);
}

// Call the function to create the form
```

```
createForm();
```

Exercise 1.2.2 Real-Time Clock:

Html File (real_time_clock.html):

```html
<!DOCTYPE html>
<html lang="en">
<head>
  <meta charset="UTF-8">
  <title> Exercise 1.2.2: Real-Time Clock</title>
</head>
<body>
  <p id="clock">
    <!-- The real-time clock will be displayed here -->
  </p>
  <script src="real_time_clock.js"></script>
</body>
</html>
```

JavaScript File(real_time_clock.js):

```javascript
// Function to update the time in the clock paragraph
function updateTime() {
    // Get the paragraph element where the time will be displayed
    const clockParagraph = document.getElementById('clock');

    // Create a new Date object to get the current date and time
    const currentDate = new Date();

    // Update the text content of the paragraph with the current time
    clockParagraph.textContent = currentDate.toLocaleString();
}

// Update the time every second using setInterval
setInterval(updateTime, 1000);
```

Exercise 1.2.3 Form Validation:

Html File (form_validation.html):

```html
<!DOCTYPE html>
<html lang="en">
<head>
    <meta charset="UTF-8">
    <title>Exercise 1.2.3: Form Validation</title>
</head>
<body>
    <form id="validationForm">
        <label for="name">Name:</label><br>
        <input type="text" id="name" name="name"><br>
        <label for="address">Address:</label><br>
        <input type="text" id="address" name="address"><br>
        <label for="email">Email:</label><br>
        <input type="email" id="email" name="email"><br>
        <button type="submit">Submit</button>
        <div id="error" style="color: red;"></div>
    </form>
    <script src="form_validation.js"></script>
</body>
</html>
```

JavaScript File(form_validation.js):

```javascript
// Function to validate the form submission
function validateForm(event) {
    // Prevent the default form submission behavior
    event.preventDefault();

    // Get the values of the name, address, and email fields
    const name = document.getElementById('name').value;
    const address = document.getElementById('address').value;
    const email = document.getElementById('email').value;
```

```javascript
    // Get the error div element
    const errorDiv = document.getElementById('error');

    // Clear any previous error messages
    errorDiv.innerHTML = '';

    // Check if any field is empty
    if (name === '' || address === '' || email === '') {
        // If any field is empty, display an error message
        errorDiv.textContent = 'All fields are required!';
    } else {
        // If all fields are filled, log a success message
        console.log('Form submitted successfully!');
        // Here you would typically submit the form data to the server
    }
}


    // Add an event listener to the form for the submit event
    document.getElementById('validationForm').addEventListener('submit', validateForm);
```

Exercise 1.2.4 Slideshow Functionality

Html File (slideshow_functionality.html):

```html
<!DOCTYPE html>
<html lang="en">
<head>
  <meta charset="UTF-8">
  <title>Exercise 1.2.4: Slideshow Functionality</title>
  <style>
    /* CSS styles for slideshow */
    #slideshow {
      width: 600px;
      height: 400px;
```

```css
    margin: 0 auto;
    overflow: hidden;
    position: relative;
    border: 1px solid #ccc;
}

.slide {
    display: none;
    width: 100%;
    height: 100%;
    position: absolute;
    top: 0;
    left: 0;
}

.prev, .next {
    cursor: pointer;
    position: absolute;
    top: 50%;
    transform: translateY(-50%);
    background-color: rgba(0, 0, 0, 0.5);
    color: white;
    font-size: 24px;
    padding: 10px;
    border: none;
    z-index: 100;
}

.prev {
    left: 0;
}
```

```
      .next {
          right: 0;
      }
   </style>
</head>
<body>
   <div id="slideshow">
      <!-- Example images -->
      <img class="slide" src="example1.jpg" alt="Image 1">
      <img class="slide" src="example2.jpg" alt="Image 2">
      <img class="slide" src="example3.jpg" alt="Image 3">
      <!-- Navigation buttons -->
      <button class="prev" onclick="prevSlide()">&#10094;</button>
      <button class="next" onclick="nextSlide()">&#10095;</button>
   </div>
   <script src="slideshow_functionality.js"></script>
</body>
</html>
```

JavaScript File (slideshow_functionality.js):

```javascript
// Initialize slide index
let slideIndex = 0;


// Get all slide elements
const slides = document.getElementsByClassName("slide");


// Function to display slides
function showSlides() {
   // Hide all slides
   for (let i = 0; i < slides.length; i++) {
      slides[i].style.display = "none";
   }
   // Increment slide index
```

```javascript
    slideIndex++;
    // Reset slide index if it exceeds the number of slides
    if (slideIndex > slides.length) {
        slideIndex = 1
    }
    // Display the current slide
    slides[slideIndex - 1].style.display = "block";
    // Call the showSlides function recursively after 2 seconds
    setTimeout(showSlides, 2000); // Change image every 2 seconds
}


// Function to show the next slide
function nextSlide() {
    // Increment slide index
    if (slideIndex < slides.length) {
        slideIndex++;
    } else {
        // Reset slide index if it exceeds the number of slides
        slideIndex = 1;
    }
    // Display the current slide
    showSlides();
}


// Function to show the previous slide
function prevSlide() {
    // Decrement slide index
    if (slideIndex > 1) {
        slideIndex--;
    } else {
        // Set slide index to the last slide if it's the first slide
        slideIndex = slides.length;
```

```
            }
            // Display the current slide
            showSlides();
        }


        // Start the slideshow
        showSlides();
```

Exercise 1.2.5 Content Loading

Html File (content_loading.html):

```html
<!DOCTYPE html>
<html lang="en">
<head>
    <meta charset="UTF-8">
    <title>Exercise 1.2.5: Content Loading</title>
</head>
<body>
    <div id="contentSection">
        <h2>Dynamic Content</h2>
        <!-- Data will be displayed dynamically here -->
    </div>


    <script src="content_loading.js"></script>
</body>
</html>
```

JavaScript File(content_loading.js):

```javascript
        // Array of products data
        const products = [
            {
                id: 1,
                name: 'Laptop',
                brand: 'Dell',
```

```javascript
    price: 799.99,
    description: 'A powerful laptop with high performance and long battery life.'
  },
  {
    id: 2,
    name: 'Smartphone',
    brand: 'Apple',
    price: 999.99,
    description: 'The latest smartphone with a stunning display and advanced camera features.'
  },
  {
    id: 3,
    name: 'Headphones',
    brand: 'Sony',
    price: 149.99,
    description: 'Wireless headphones with noise cancellation and long-lasting comfort.'
  }
];


// Get the content section element
const contentSection = document.getElementById('contentSection');


// Loop through products array and create HTML for each product
products.forEach(product => {
  const productDiv = document.createElement('div');
  // Populate the product information in HTML
  productDiv.innerHTML = `
    <h3>${product.name}</h3>
    <p><strong>Brand:</strong> ${product.brand}</p>
    <p><strong>Price:</strong> $${product.price}</p>
    <p><strong>Description:</strong> ${product.description}</p>
```

```
      <hr>
    `;
      // Append the product HTML to the content section
      contentSection.appendChild(productDiv);
    });
```

Exercise 1.2.6 Drag elements:

Html File (drag.html):

```html
<!DOCTYPE html>
<html lang="en">
<head>
  <meta charset="UTF-8">
  <title> Exercise 1.2.6: Drag Elements Inside Box</title>
  <style>
    /* CSS styles for drag elements */
    #container {
      width: 400px;
      height: 300px;
      border: 2px solid #ccc;
      padding: 10px;
      margin: 50px auto;
      position: relative;
    }

    .draggable {
      width: 100px;
      height: 50px;
      background-color: #f0f0f0;
      border: 1px solid #999;
      border-radius: 5px;
      padding: 10px;
      cursor: pointer;
      position: absolute;
```

```html
      }
    </style>
  </head>
  <body>
    <div id="container">
      <div class="draggable" style="top: 50px; left: 50px;">Drag me</div>
      <div class="draggable" style="top: 120px; left: 120px;">Drag me too</div>
      <!-- Add more draggable elements here -->
    </div>
    <script src="drag.js"></script>
  </body>
</html>
```

JavaScript File(drag.js):

```javascript
document.addEventListener('DOMContentLoaded', function () {
    const container = document.getElementById('container');
    const draggables = document.querySelectorAll('.draggable');
    let activeDraggable = null;

    // Add mousedown event listener to each draggable element
    draggables.forEach(draggable => {
      draggable.addEventListener('mousedown', function (e) {
        activeDraggable = this;
        // Calculate offset between mouse pointer and draggable element
        const offsetX = e.clientX - activeDraggable.getBoundingClientRect().left;
        const offsetY = e.clientY - activeDraggable.getBoundingClientRect().top;

        // Add mousemove and mouseup event listeners to the document
        document.addEventListener('mousemove', drag);
        document.addEventListener('mouseup', release);

        // Drag function to move the draggable element
        function drag(e) {
```

```javascript
      const x = e.clientX - offsetX;
      const y = e.clientY - offsetY;

      // Ensure the draggable element stays within the container
      const maxX = container.offsetWidth - activeDraggable.offsetWidth;
      const maxY = container.offsetHeight - activeDraggable.offsetHeight;
      const boundedX = Math.min(maxX, Math.max(0, x));
      const boundedY = Math.min(maxY, Math.max(0, y));

      activeDraggable.style.left = boundedX + 'px';
      activeDraggable.style.top = boundedY + 'px';
    }

    // Release function to stop dragging when mouse is released
    function release() {
      document.removeEventListener('mousemove', drag);
      document.removeEventListener('mouseup', release);
      activeDraggable = null;
    }
  });

  // Prevent default drag behavior for draggable elements
  draggable.addEventListener('dragstart', function (e) {
    e.preventDefault();
  });
  });
});
```

Exercise 1.2.7 Search Functionality

Html File (dynamic_search.html):

```html
<!DOCTYPE html>
<html lang="en">
<head>
```

```html
<meta charset="UTF-8">
<title>Exercise 1.2.7: Dynamic Search</title>
<style>
    /* CSS styles for search functionality */
    body {
        font-family: Arial, sans-serif;
    }

    ul {
        list-style-type: none;
        padding: 0;
    }

    li {
        padding: 10px;
        border-bottom: 1px solid #ccc;
    }

    li:last-child {
        border-bottom: none;
    }
</style>
</head>
<body>
    <input type="text" id="searchInput" placeholder="Search...">
    <ul id="resultsList"></ul>
    <script src="dynamic_search.js"></script>
</body>
</html>
```

JavaScript File(dynamic_search.js):

```javascript
const items = [
    'Apple',
```

```javascript
  'Banana',
  'Orange',
  'Mango',
  'Pineapple',
  'Grapes',
  'Watermelon',
  'Kiwi',
  'Strawberry',
  'Blueberry'
];
const searchInput = document.getElementById('searchInput');
const resultsList = document.getElementById('resultsList');
// Function to filter items based on user input
function filterItems(query) {
  const filteredItems = items.filter(item =>
item.toLowerCase().includes(query.toLowerCase()));
  displayResults(filteredItems);
}
// Function to display filtered results
function displayResults(filteredItems) {
  resultsList.innerHTML = '';
  filteredItems.forEach(item => {
    const li = document.createElement('li');
    li.textContent = item;
    resultsList.appendChild(li);
  });
}

// Event listener for input changes in the search input field
searchInput.addEventListener('input', () => {
  const query = searchInput.value;
  filterItems(query);
```

```
});
```

Exercise 1.2.8 Simple Calculator

Html File (simple_calculator.html):

```html
<!DOCTYPE html>
<html lang="en">
<head>
  <meta charset="UTF-8">
  <title>Exercise 1.2.8: Simple Calculator</title>
  <style>
    /* CSS styles for simple calculator */
    label {
      display: block;
      margin-bottom: 5px;
    }

    input[type="number"] {
      width: 200px;
      margin-bottom: 10px;
    }

    select {
      width: 200px;
      margin-bottom: 10px;
    }

    button {
      padding: 8px 16px;
      background-color: #4CAF50;
      color: white;
      border: none;
      border-radius: 4px;
      cursor: pointer;
```

```html
                }

            button:hover {
                background-color: #45a049;
            }
        </style>
    </head>
    <body>
        <h2>Simple Calculator</h2>
        <label for="num1">Enter first number:</label>
        <input type="number" id="num1">
        <label for="num2">Enter second number:</label>
        <input type="number" id="num2">
        <label for="operation">Choose an operation:</label>
        <select id="operation">
            <option value="+">Addition</option>
            <option value="-">Subtraction</option>
            <option value="*">Multiplication</option>
            <option value="/">Division</option>
        </select>
        <button onclick="calculate()">Calculate</button>
        <p id="result"></p>
        <script src="simple_calculator.js"></script>
    </body>
</html>
```

JavaScript File(simple_calculator.js):

```javascript
// Function to perform calculation based on user input
function calculate() {
    const num1 = parseFloat(document.getElementById('num1').value);
    const num2 = parseFloat(document.getElementById('num2').value);
    const operation = document.getElementById('operation').value;
    let result;
```

```javascript
    // Perform calculation based on selected operation
    switch (operation) {
        case '+':
            result = num1 + num2;
            break;
        case '-':
            result = num1 - num2;
            break;
        case '*':
            result = num1 * num2;
            break;
        case '/':
            result = num1 / num2;
            break;
        default:
            result = 'Invalid operation';
    }


    // Display the result
    document.getElementById('result').textContent = `Result: ${result}`;
}
```

Exercise 1.2.9 Smooth Scrolling

Html File (smooth_scrolling.html):

```html
<!DOCTYPE html>
<html lang="en">
<head>
  <meta charset="UTF-8">
  <title>Exercise 1.2.9: Scroll to Section</title>
  <style>
    /* CSS styles for smooth scrolling */
    body {
```

```css
        font-family: Arial, sans-serif;
        margin: 0;
        padding: 0;
    }

    header {
        background-color: #333;
        color: #fff;
        padding: 10px;
        text-align: center;
    }

    nav {
        display: flex;
        justify-content: center;
        margin-bottom: 20px;
    }

        nav a {
            text-decoration: none;
            margin: 0 10px;
            color: #fff;
        }

    section {
        padding: 20px;
        margin: 20px 0;
        border: 1px solid #ccc;
    }
    </style>
</head>
<body>
```

```html
<header>
    <h1>Scroll to Section</h1>
</header>
<nav>
    <a href="#section1">Product Description</a>
    <a href="#section2">Customer Reviews</a>
    <a href="#section3">Related Products</a>
</nav>
<section id="section1">
    <h2>Product Description</h2>
    <p>This section provides detailed information about our featured product.</p>
</section>
<section id="section2">
    <h2>Customer Reviews</h2>
    <p>Here you can find reviews from our customers who have purchased this
product.</p>
</section>
<section id="section3">
    <h2>Related Products</h2>
        <p>Here, you can find similar products.</p>
</section>
<script src="smooth_scrolling.js"></script>
</body>
</html>
```

JavaScript File(smooth_scrolling.js):

```javascript
// Smooth scrolling functionality
document.querySelectorAll('a[href^="#"]').forEach(anchor => {
    anchor.addEventListener('click', function (e) {
        e.preventDefault();

        const target = document.querySelector(this.getAttribute('href'));
```

```
    // Smooth scroll to the target section
    window.scrollTo({
        top: target.offsetTop,
        behavior: 'smooth'
    });
  });
});
```

Exercise 1.2.10 Dropdown Menu

Html File (dropdown_menu.html):

```html
<!DOCTYPE html>
<html lang="en">
<head>
  <meta charset="UTF-8">
  <title>Exercise 1.2.10: Dropdown Menu</title>
  <style>
    /* CSS styles for dropdown menu */
    .dropdown {
      position: relative;
      display: inline-block;
    }

    .dropdown-content {
      display: none;
      position: absolute;
      background-color: #f9f9f9;
      min-width: 160px;
      box-shadow: 0px 8px 16px 0px rgba(0,0,0,0.2);
      z-index: 1;
    }

      .dropdown-content a {
        color: black;
```

```
        padding: 12px 16px;
        text-decoration: none;
        display: block;
    }


        .dropdown-content a:hover {
          background-color: #f1f1f1;
        }


    .dropdown:hover .dropdown-content {
      display: block;
    }
  </style>
</head>
<body>
  <div class="dropdown">
    <button class="dropbtn">Dropdown</button>
    <div class="dropdown-content">
      <a href="#">Option 1</a>
      <a href="#">Option 2</a>
      <a href="#">Option 3</a>
    </div>
  </div>


  <script src="dropdown_menu.js"></script>
</body>
</html>
```

JavaScript File(dropdown_menu.js):

```
document.addEventListener('DOMContentLoaded', function () {
  const dropdowns = document.querySelectorAll('.dropdown');

  dropdowns.forEach(dropdown => {
```

```javascript
    dropdown.addEventListener('click', function () {
        // Toggle the display of dropdown content
        this.querySelector('.dropdown-content').classList.toggle('show');
    });
});


// Close dropdowns when clicking outside of them
window.addEventListener('click', function (e) {
    dropdowns.forEach(dropdown => {
        if (!dropdown.contains(e.target)) {
            dropdown.querySelector('.dropdown-content').classList.remove('show');
        }
    });
});
});
```

Exercise 1.2.11

Html File :

```html
<!DOCTYPE html>
<html lang="en">
<head>
    <meta charset="UTF-8">
    <title>Exercise 1.2.11: Dynamic Table</title>
    <style>
        /* CSS for table borders */
        table {
            border-collapse: collapse;
            width: 100%;
        }

        th, td {
            border: 1px solid #dddddd;
            text-align: left;
```

```css
      padding: 8px;
    }

    th {
      background-color: #f2f2f2;
    }
  </style>
</head>
<body>
  <h2>Dynamic Table</h2>
  <div id="tableContainer"></div>
  <script src="dynamic_table.js"></script>
</body>
</html>
```

JavaScript File (dynamic_table.js):

```javascript
document.addEventListener('DOMContentLoaded', function () {
  // Sample array of objects with real data
  const data = [
    { name: "John Doe", age: 30, city: "New York" },
    { name: "Jane Smith", age: 25, city: "Los Angeles" },
    { name: "Michael Johnson", age: 35, city: "Chicago" }
  ];

  const tableContainer = document.getElementById('tableContainer');

  // Function to generate and display the dynamic table
  function generateTable(data) {
    const table = document.createElement('table');
    const headers = Object.keys(data[0]);

    // Create table headers
    const headerRow = document.createElement('tr');
```

```javascript
  headers.forEach(headerText => {
    const header = document.createElement('th');
    header.textContent = headerText;
    headerRow.appendChild(header);
  });
  table.appendChild(headerRow);

  // Create table rows with data
  data.forEach(item => {
    const row = document.createElement('tr');
    headers.forEach(header => {
      const cell = document.createElement('td');
      cell.textContent = item[header];
      row.appendChild(cell);
    });
    table.appendChild(row);
  });

  tableContainer.appendChild(table);
}

// Generate and display the table
generateTable(data);
});
```

Exercise 1.2.12

Html File:

```html
<!DOCTYPE html>
<html lang="en">
<head>
  <meta charset="UTF-8">
  <title>Exercise 1.2.12: Quiz Application</title>
  <style>
```

```css
/* CSS styles */
body {
    font-family: Arial, sans-serif;
}

.quiz-container {
    max-width: 600px;
    margin: 0 auto;
    padding: 20px;
    border: 1px solid #ccc;
    border-radius: 5px;
}

.question {
    margin-bottom: 20px;
}

.options label {
    display: block;
    margin-bottom: 10px;
}

.feedback {
    font-weight: bold;
    margin-top: 10px;
}
```
```html
    </style>
</head>
<body>
    <div class="quiz-container">
        <div class="question">
            <p>1. What is the capital of France?</p>
```

```html
      <div class="options">
         <label><input type="radio" name="q1" value="a"> a) London</label>
         <label><input type="radio" name="q1" value="b"> b) Paris</label>
         <label><input type="radio" name="q1" value="c"> c) Rome</label>
      </div>
   </div>
   <div class="question">
      <p>2. What is the largest planet in our solar system?</p>
      <div class="options">
         <label><input type="radio" name="q2" value="a"> a) Jupiter</label>
         <label><input type="radio" name="q2" value="b"> b) Saturn</label>
         <label><input type="radio" name="q2" value="c"> c) Earth</label>
      </div>
   </div>
   <div class="question">
      <p>3. Who developed the theory of relativity?</p>
      <div class="options">
         <label><input type="radio" name="q3" value="a"> a) Isaac Newton</label>
         <label><input type="radio" name="q3" value="b"> b) Albert Einstein</label>
         <label><input type="radio" name="q3" value="c"> c) Galileo Galilei</label>
      </div>
   </div>
   <button onclick="submitQuiz()">Submit</button>
   <div id="quizFeedback" class="feedback"></div>
</div>
<script src="quiz_application.js"></script>
</body>
</html>
```

JavaScript File (quiz_application.js):

```javascript
function submitQuiz() {
    const answers = {
        q1: document.querySelector('input[name="q1"]:checked'),
```

```javascript
      q2: document.querySelector('input[name="q2"]:checked'),
      q3: document.querySelector('input[name="q3"]:checked')
};

let score = 0;
let feedback = '';

// Check answers and calculate score
if (answers.q1 && answers.q1.value === 'b') {
    score++;
}
if (answers.q2 && answers.q2.value === 'a') {
    score++;
}
if (answers.q3 && answers.q3.value === 'b') {
    score++;
}

// Generate feedback based on score
switch (score) {
    case 0:
        feedback = 'You scored 0 out of 4. Better luck next time!';
        break;
    case 1:
        feedback = 'You scored 1 out of 4. Keep learning!';
        break;
    case 2:
        feedback = 'You scored 2 out of 4. Good job!';
        break;
    case 3:
        feedback = 'You scored 3 out of 4. Excellent!';
        break;
```

```
    }

    // Display feedback
    document.getElementById('quizFeedback').textContent = feedback;
}
```

Chapter 2
Student Management System using JavaScript

2 Student Management System

2.1 Exercise

Exercise: Develop a Student Management System using HTML, CSS, and JavaScript.

Description: Create a web-based application that facilitates the management of student records. Each student record should contain information such as name, age, and grade. Users should be able to perform various operations on these records, including adding, editing, and removing students. Additionally, the system should support sorting students by grade, name, and age. Users should also have the ability to search for students based on their name, grade, or age. Finally, the system should display the list of students with their corresponding details (see Figure1: User Interface example).

Requirements:

1. Each student record should include fields for name, age, and grade.
2. Users should be able to add new student records through a user-friendly interface.
3. Users should have the ability to edit existing student records, allowing them to update name, age, and grade.
4. Users should be able to remove student records from the system.
5. The system should provide functionality to sort students by grade, name, and age.
6. Users should be able to search for students by their name, grade, or age, with the search results displayed dynamically.
7. The list of students should be displayed prominently on the interface, presenting all relevant details clearly.

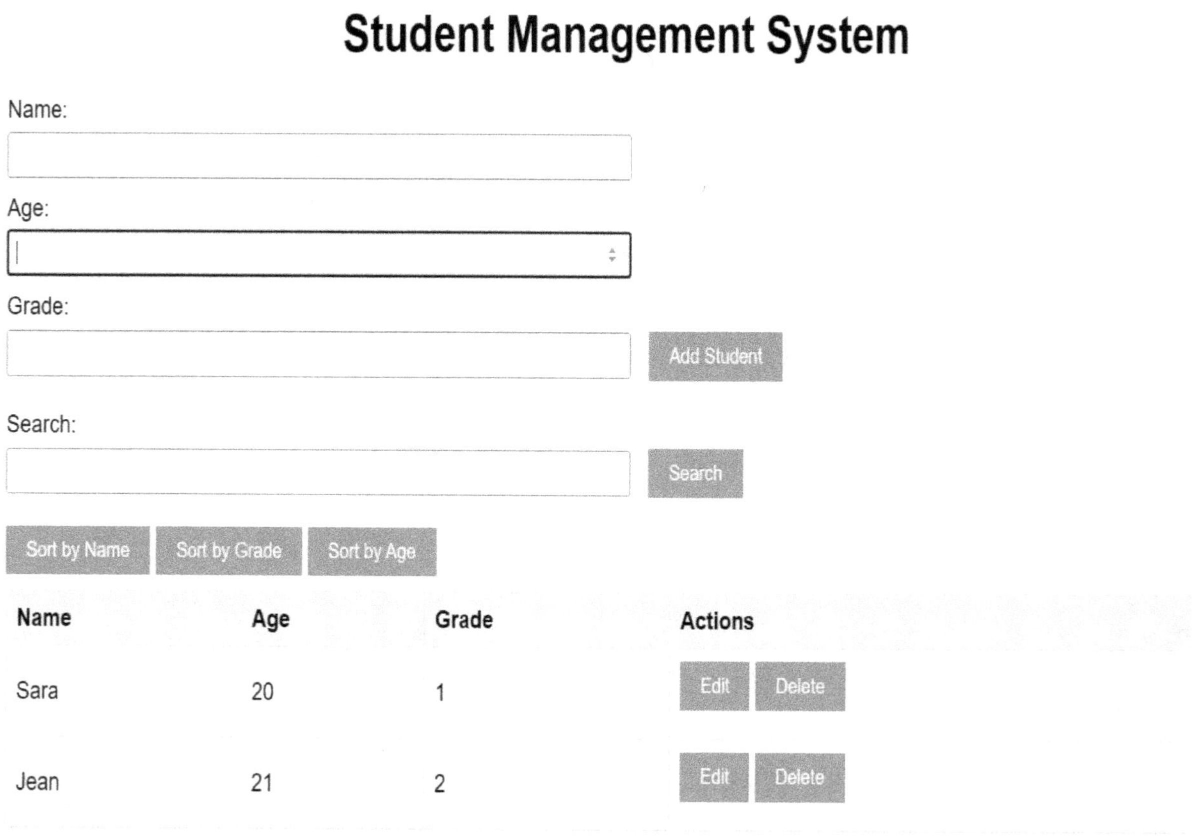

Student Management System

Name:

[   ]

Age:

[⇕]

Grade:

[   ] [Add Student]

Search:

[   ] [Search]

[Sort by Name] [Sort by Grade] [Sort by Age]

Name	Age	Grade	Actions
Sara	20	1	[Edit] [Delete]
Jean	21	2	[Edit] [Delete]

Figure 2.1 User interface example (Student Management System)

2.2 Solution

Student management system

Html File (Student_Management.html):

```html
<!DOCTYPE html>
<html lang="en">
<head>
    <meta charset="UTF-8">
    <meta name="viewport" content="width=device-width, initial-scale=1.0">
    <title>Student Management System</title>
    <style>
        /* CSS styles */
        body {
            font-family: Arial, sans-serif;
            margin: 0;
            padding: 20px;
        }

        h1 {
            text-align: center;
        }

        form {
            margin-bottom: 10px;
        }

        label {
            display: block;
            margin-bottom: 5px;
        }

        input[type="text"],
        input[type="number"] {
```

```css
    width: calc(50% - 10px); /* Adjusted width to half of the container with spacing */
    padding: 5px;
    margin-bottom: 10px;
    margin-right: 10px;
}

input[type="text"]:last-child,
input[type="number"]:last-child {
    margin-right: 0;
}

button {
    padding: 8px 16px;
    background-color: #4CAF50;
    color: white;
    border: none;
    cursor: pointer;
    margin-bottom: 10px;
}

button:hover {
    background-color: #45a049;
}

table {
    width: 100%;
    border-collapse: collapse;
    margin-bottom: 20px;
}

th, td {
    border: 1px solid #ddd;
```

```html
        padding: 8px;
        text-align: left;
      }

      th {
        background-color: #f2f2f2;
      }
    </style>
  </head>
  <body>
    <h1>Student Management System</h1>

    <!-- Form to add new student -->
    <form id="addForm">
      <label for="name">Name:</label>
      <input type="text" id="name" name="name" required>
      <label for="age">Age:</label>
      <input type="number" id="age" name="age" required>
      <label for="grade">Grade:</label>
      <input type="text" id="grade" name="grade" required>
      <button type="submit">Add Student</button>
    </form>

    <!-- Form to search students -->
    <form id="searchForm">
      <label for="search">Search:</label>
      <input type="text" id="search" name="search">
      <button type="submit">Search</button>
    </form>

    <!-- Sort buttons -->
    <button id="sortByName">Sort by Name</button>
```

```html
<button id="sortByGrade">Sort by Grade</button>
<button id="sortByAge">Sort by Age</button>

<!-- Display area for student list (changed from ul to table) -->
<table id="studentList">
  <thead>
    <tr>
      <th>Name</th>
      <th>Age</th>
      <th>Grade</th>
      <th>Actions</th> <!-- Added Actions column for edit and delete buttons -->
    </tr>
  </thead>
  <tbody></tbody>
</table>
<script src="Student_Management.js"></script>
</body>
</html>
```

JavaScript File (Student_Management.js):

```javascript
// Array to store students
let students = [];

// Function to add a new student to the array
function addStudent(name, age, grade) {
  students.push({ name, age, grade });
}

// Function to display all students
function displayStudents() {
  const studentList = document.querySelector('#studentList tbody');
  studentList.innerHTML = ''; // Clear previous content
  students.forEach((student, index) => {
```

```javascript
    const row = document.createElement('tr');
    row.innerHTML = `
                <td>${student.name}</td>
                <td>${student.age}</td>
                <td>${student.grade}</td>
                <td>
                    <button class="editBtn" data-index="${index}">Edit</button>
                    <button class="removeBtn" data-index="${index}">Delete</button>
                </td>
            `;
    studentList.appendChild(row);
  });
  // Add event listeners to dynamically created edit and remove buttons
  const editButtons = document.querySelectorAll('.editBtn');
  editButtons.forEach(button => {
    button.addEventListener('click', function () {
      const index = parseInt(button.getAttribute('data-index'));
      editStudent(index);
    });
  });
  const removeButtons = document.querySelectorAll('.removeBtn');
  removeButtons.forEach(button => {
    button.addEventListener('click', function () {
      const index = parseInt(button.getAttribute('data-index'));
      removeStudent(index);
    });
  });
}

// Function to edit a student
function editStudent(index) {
  const student = students[index];
```

```javascript
    const newName = prompt(`Enter new name for ${student.name}:`, student.name);
    const newAge = prompt(`Enter new age for ${student.name}:`, student.age);
    const newGrade = prompt(`Enter new grade for ${student.name}:`, student.grade);
    if (newName !== null && newAge !== null && newGrade !== null) {
        students[index] = { name: newName, age: newAge, grade: newGrade };
        displayStudents(); // Update the display after editing
    }
}


// Function to remove a student
function removeStudent(index) {
    if (index >= 0 && index < students.length) {
        students.splice(index, 1);
        displayStudents(); // Update the display after removing
    } else {
        alert('Invalid index!');
    }
}


// Event listener for add form submission
const addForm = document.getElementById('addForm');
addForm.addEventListener('submit', function (event) {
    event.preventDefault(); // Prevent default form submission
    const name = addForm.name.value;
    const age = addForm.age.value;
    const grade = addForm.grade.value;
    addStudent(name, age, grade);
    displayStudents(); // Update the display with the new student
    addForm.reset(); // Clear the form fields after submission
});


// Event listener for search form submission
```

```javascript
const searchForm = document.getElementById('searchForm');
searchForm.addEventListener('submit', function (event) {
    event.preventDefault(); // Prevent default form submission
    const searchQuery = searchForm.search.value;
    const results = searchStudents(searchQuery);
    displayStudents(results); // Display search results
    searchForm.reset(); // Clear the search form field after submission
});

// Function to search for students based on a query
function searchStudents(query) {
    return students.filter(student =>
        student.name.toLowerCase().includes(query.toLowerCase()) ||
        student.grade.toLowerCase() === query.toLowerCase() ||
        student.age == query
    );
}

// Function to sort students by name
function sortStudentsByName() {
    students.sort((a, b) => a.name.localeCompare(b.name));
    displayStudents(); // Update the display after sorting
}

// Function to sort students by grade
function sortStudentsByGrade() {
    students.sort((a, b) => a.grade.localeCompare(b.grade));
    displayStudents(); // Update the display after sorting
}

// Function to sort students by age
function sortStudentsByAge() {
```

```javascript
    students.sort((a, b) => a.age - b.age);
    displayStudents(); // Update the display after sorting
}


// Event listeners for sort buttons
document.getElementById('sortByName').addEventListener('click',
sortStudentsByName);
document.getElementById('sortByGrade').addEventListener('click',
sortStudentsByGrade);
document.getElementById('sortByAge').addEventListener('click', sortStudentsByAge);
```

Chapter 3

jQuery

3 jQuery

3.1 Exercises

Exercise 3.1 Todo List

Create a simple Todo List application using jQuery. The application should allow users to add new tasks, and mark tasks as completed (Example: Figure 3.1).

Todo List

Add New Todo

Sport

Shopping

~~Meeting~~

Figure 3.1. Todo list

Exercise 3.2 Real-Time Search Filter with jQuery

Create a real-time search filter for a list of items using jQuery. The filter should allow users to dynamically filter the list items based on their search query (Example: Figure 3.2).

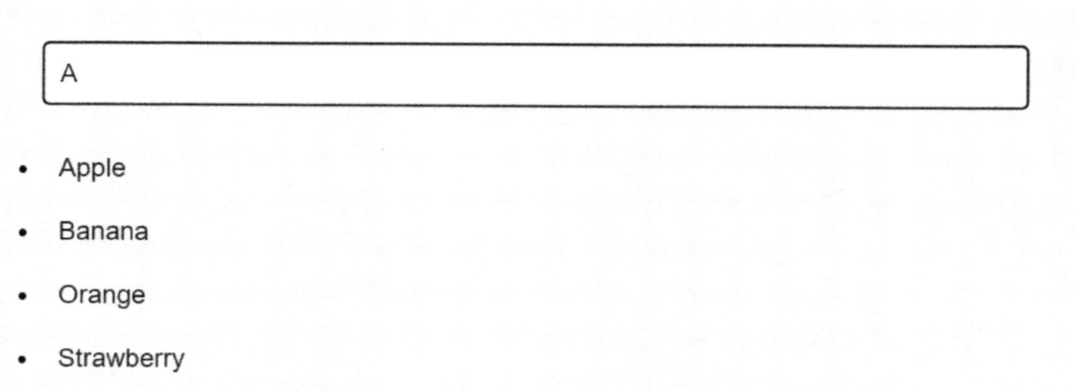

A

- Apple
- Banana
- Orange
- Strawberry

Figure 3.2 Search Filter

Exercise 3.3 Pagination System

Implement a pagination system for a list of countries displayed on a webpage. Each page should display a maximum of 5 countries. When a user clicks on a pagination link, the corresponding countries for that page should be displayed while hiding the rest (Example: Figure 3.3).

Figure 3.3 Pagination System

Exercise 3.4 Sortable table columns

Create a sortable table with three columns: "Name", "Age", and "Country". Implement sorting functionality using jQuery. Clicking on any column header should toggle between ascending and descending sorting based on the values in that column (Example: Figure 3.4).

Name	Age	Country
Alice	30	UK
John	25	USA
Bob	20	Canada

Figure 3.4. Sortable table columns

Exercise 3.5 Form Validation

Create a form with input fields for name, email, and password. Use jQuery to validate the form fields. Check if the name field is not empty, the email field follows a valid email format, and the password is at least 8 characters long (Example: Figure 3.5).

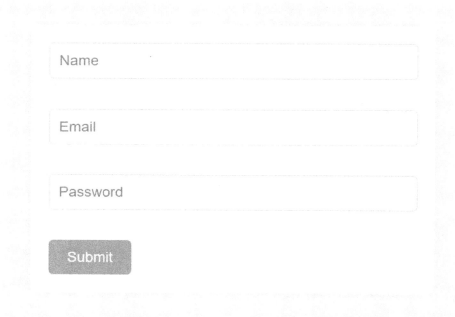

Figure 3.5 Form Validation

Exercise 3.6 Navbar

Create a web page for a product store with a navigation bar. Implement dynamic content loading based on the selected menu item (Example: Figure 3.6).

Figure 3.6 Navbar

Exercise 3.7 Authentication Page

Implement simple Authentication page using jQuery (Example: Figure 3.7)

Figure 3.7 Authentication Page

Exercise 3.8 Ajax (Get request)

Implement a feature where a user can type a search query into an input field, and upon pressing Enter or clicking a button, jQuery sends an AJAX request to fetch search results from an API (like GitHub). Display the results on the page (Example: Figure 3.8).

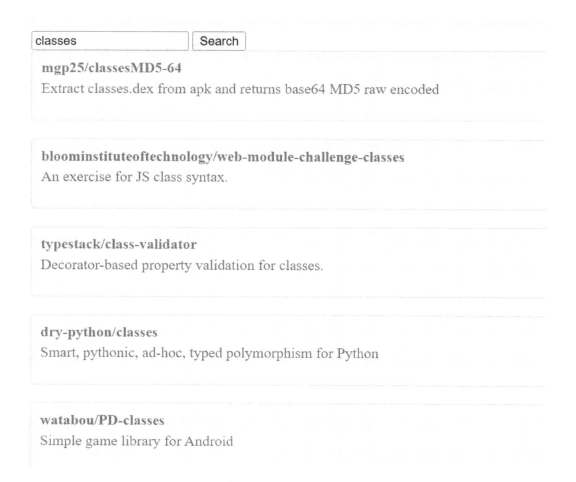

Figure 3.8 GitHub Repository Search using AJAX Get request

Exercise 3.9 Ajax (Post request)

Create a form that sends a POST request using jQuery AJAX, demonstrating the submission of user data (Example: Figure 3.9).

Figure 3.9 Ajax Post Request

Exercise *3*.10 A*jax* Data Visualization

Create a web page that displays a line chart visualizing temperature data for the past week. The chart should show the average temperature (in Celsius) for each day (Example: Figure 3.10).

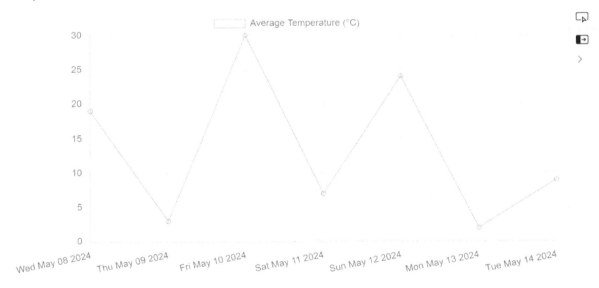

Figure 3.10 Average temperature by day

Exercise 3.11 Carousel Slider

Build a carousel slider using jQuery to display a set of images or content in a slideshow format. Implement features such as automatic sliding, and navigation arrows (Example: Figure 3.11).

Figure 3.11 Carousel Slider

3.2 Solutions

Exercise 3.1 Todo List

Html File:

```html
<!DOCTYPE html>
<html lang="en">
<head>
  <meta charset="UTF-8">
  <meta name="viewport" content="width=device-width, initial-scale=1.0">
  <title>Exercise 3.1</title>
  <style>
    /* Reset CSS */
    body, ul {
      margin: 0;
      padding: 0;
    }

    body {
      font-family: Arial, sans-serif;
      background-color: #f2f2f2;
    }

    .container {
      max-width: 400px;
      margin: 50px auto;
      background-color: #fff;
      padding: 20px;
      border-radius: 8px;
      box-shadow: 0 0 10px rgba(0, 0, 0, 0.1);
    }
```

```css
h1 {
    text-align: center;
    margin-bottom: 20px;
}

input[type="text"] {
    width: calc(100% - 20px);
    padding: 10px;
    font-size: 16px;
    border: 1px solid #ddd;
    border-radius: 4px;
}

    input[type="text"]:focus {
        outline: none;
        border-color: #3498db;
    }

ul {
    list-style: none;
    padding: 0;
}

li {
    padding: 10px;
    border-bottom: 1px solid #ddd;
    cursor: pointer;
}

    li:last-child {
        border-bottom: none;
    }
```

```html
    .completed {
        text-decoration: line-through;
        color: #999;
    }
</style>
</head>
<body>
    <div class="container">
        <h1>Todo List</h1>
        <!-- Input field for adding new tasks -->
        <input type="text" id="new-todo" placeholder="Add New Todo">
        <!-- Unordered list to contain the list of tasks -->
        <ul id="todo-list"></ul>
    </div>
    <script src="https://code.jquery.com/jquery-3.6.0.min.js"></script>
    <script src="Todo_List.js">    </script>
</body>
</html>
```

JavaScript File (Todo_List.js):

```javascript
$(document).ready(function () {
    // Event handler for when a key is pressed in the new todo input field
    $('#new-todo').keypress(function (event) {
        // Check if the key pressed is the Enter key (key code 13)
        if (event.which === 13) {
            // Get the text entered in the input field
            var todoText = $(this).val();
            // Clear the input field
            $(this).val('');
            // Prepend a new todo item to the todo list
            $('#todo-list').prepend('<li>' + todoText + '</li>');
        }
```

```
        });

        // Event handler for when a todo item is clicked
        $('#todo-list').on('click', 'li', function () {
            // Toggle the completed class on the clicked todo item
            $(this).toggleClass('completed');
        });
    });
```

Exercise 3.2 Real-Time Search Filter with jQuery

Html File:

```html
<!DOCTYPE html>
<html lang="en">
<head>
    <meta charset="UTF-8">
    <meta name="viewport" content="width=device-width, initial-scale=1.0">
    <title>Exercise 3.2</title>
    <style>
        /* Reset CSS */
        body, ul {
            margin: 0;
            padding: 0;
        }

        body {
            font-family: Arial, sans-serif;
            background-color: #f2f2f2;
        }

        .container {
            max-width: 600px;
            margin: 50px auto;
        }
```

```css
        input[type="text"] {
            width: 100%;
            padding: 10px;
            font-size: 16px;
            border: 1px solid #ddd;
            border-radius: 4px;
            margin-bottom: 20px;
        }

        .list-item {
            padding: 10px;
            border-bottom: 1px solid #ddd;
        }

            .list-item:last-child {
                border-bottom: none;
            }
    </style>
</head>
<body>
    <div class="container">
        <!-- Input field for search -->
        <input type="text" id="search" placeholder="Search...">
        <!-- List of items to be filtered -->
        <ul id="list">
            <li class="list-item">Apple</li>
            <li class="list-item">Banana</li>
            <li class="list-item">Orange</li>
            <li class="list-item">Strawberry</li>
            <!-- Add more list items as needed -->
        </ul>
```

```html
    </div>
    <script src="https://code.jquery.com/jquery-3.6.0.min.js"></script>
    <script src="Search_Filter.js">   </script>
</body>
</html>
```

JavaScript File (Search_Filter.js):

```javascript
$(document).ready(function () {

    // Event handler for keyup event on the search input field
    $('#search').keyup(function () {
        // Get the value entered in the search input field
        var searchText = $(this).val().toLowerCase();
        // Filter the list items based on the search text
        $('#list .list-item').each(function () {
            var listItemText = $(this).text().toLowerCase();
            if (listItemText.indexOf(searchText) === -1) {
                // Hide list items that do not match the search text
                $(this).hide();
            } else {
                // Show list items that match the search text
                $(this).show();
            }
        });
    });

});
```

Exercise 3.3 Pagination System

Html File:

```html
<!DOCTYPE html>
<html lang="en">
<head>
```

```html
<meta charset="UTF-8">
<meta name="viewport" content="width=device-width, initial-scale=1.0">
<title>Exercise 3.3</title>
<style>
  /* CSS styles */
  body {
    font-family: Arial, sans-serif;
    background-color: #f2f2f2;
    margin: 0;
    padding: 0;
  }

  .container {
    max-width: 600px;
    margin: 50px auto;
    background-color: #fff;
    padding: 20px;
    border-radius: 5px;
    box-shadow: 0 0 10px rgba(0, 0, 0, 0.1);
  }

  ul {
    list-style: none;
    padding: 0;
  }

  li {
    padding: 10px;
    border-bottom: 1px solid #ddd;
  }

  .page-link {
```

```css
            display: inline-block;
            padding: 5px 10px;
            background-color: #3498db;
            color: #fff;
            text-decoration: none;
            border-radius: 4px;
            margin-right: 5px;
        }

        .page-link:hover {
            background-color: #2980b9;
        }

        .current-page {
            background-color: #2980b9;
        }
    </style>
</head>
<body>
    <div class="container">
        <!-- List of items -->
        <ul id="items">
            <!-- Real list items -->
            <li>Afghanistan</li>
            <li>Albania</li>
            <li>Algeria</li>
            <li>Andorra</li>
            <li>Angola</li>
            <li>Antigua and Barbuda</li>
            <li>Argentina</li>
            <li>Armenia</li>
            <li>Australia</li>
```

```html
      <li>Austria</li>
      <li>Azerbaijan</li>
      <li>Bahamas</li>
      <li>Bahrain</li>
      <li>Bangladesh</li>
      <li>Barbados</li>
      <li>Belarus</li>
      <li>Belgium</li>
      <li>Belize</li>
      <li>Benin</li>
      <li>Bhutan</li>
    </ul>
    <!-- Pagination links -->
    <div id="pagination"></div>
  </div>
  <script src="https://code.jquery.com/jquery-3.6.0.min.js"></script>
  <script src="Pagination_System.js"></script>
</body>
</html>
```

JavaScript File (Pagination_System.js) :

```javascript
$(document).ready(function () {
    // Number of items per page
    var itemsPerPage = 5;
    // List of items
    var items = $('#items li');
    // Calculate total number of pages
    var totalPages = Math.ceil(items.length / itemsPerPage);

    // Function to display items for a given page
    function displayItems(page) {
        $('#items li').hide(); // Hide all list items
        var startIndex = (page - 1) * itemsPerPage;
```

```javascript
        var endIndex = startIndex + itemsPerPage;
        items.slice(startIndex, endIndex).show(); // Show items for the current page
    }


    // Function to generate pagination links
    function generatePaginationLinks() {
        $('#pagination').empty(); // Clear previous pagination links
        for (var i = 1; i <= totalPages; i++) {
            var linkClass = (i === 1) ? 'page-link current-page' : 'page-link'; // Set class for
current page link
            $('#pagination').append('<a href="#" class="' + linkClass + '">' + i + '</a>'); //
Create pagination link
        }
    }


    // Display items for the first page
    displayItems(1);
    // Generate pagination links
    generatePaginationLinks();


    // Event handler for clicking on pagination links
    $(document).on('click', '.page-link', function (e) {
        e.preventDefault();
        var page = parseInt($(this).text());
        displayItems(page); // Display items for the clicked page
        $('.page-link').removeClass('current-page'); // Remove 'current-page' class from all
links
        $(this).addClass('current-page'); // Add 'current-page' class to the clicked link
    });
});
```

Exercise 3.4 Sortable Table

Html File:

```html
<!DOCTYPE html>
<html lang="en">
<head>
    <meta charset="UTF-8">
    <meta name="viewport" content="width=device-width, initial-scale=1.0">
    <title>Exercise 3.4 </title>
    <style>
        /* CSS styles for the table */
        table {
            border-collapse: collapse;
            width: 50%;
            margin: 20px auto; /* Center the table */
            border: 2px solid #ddd;
        }

        th, td {
            border: 1px solid #ddd;
            text-align: left;
            padding: 8px;
        }

        th {
            cursor: pointer;
            background-color: #f2f2f2;
        }
        /* Style for the alternating row colors */
        tbody tr:nth-child(even) {
            background-color: #f2f2f2;
        }
        /* Style for hover effect on rows */
```

```
        tbody tr:hover {
            background-color: #ddd;
        }
    </style>
</head>
<body>

    <table id="sortableTable">
        <thead>
            <tr>
                <th data-sort="name">Name</th>
                <th data-sort="age">Age</th>
                <th data-sort="country">Country</th>
            </tr>
        </thead>
        <tbody>
            <tr>
                <td>John</td>
                <td>25</td>
                <td>USA</td>
            </tr>
            <tr>
                <td>Alice</td>
                <td>30</td>
                <td>UK</td>
            </tr>
            <tr>
                <td>Bob</td>
                <td>20</td>
                <td>Canada</td>
            </tr>
        </tbody>
```

```
</table>

<script src="https://ajax.googleapis.com/ajax/libs/jquery/3.5.1/jquery.min.js"></script>
<script src="Sorting_Table.js"></script>
</body>
</html>
```

JavaScript File (Sorting_Table.js)

```javascript
$(document).ready(function () {
    $("#sortableTable th").click(function () {
        var table = $(this).parents('table').eq(0);
        var rows = table.find('tr:gt(0)').toArray().sort(compare($(this).index()));
        this.asc = !this.asc;
        if (!this.asc) {
            rows = rows.reverse();
        }
        for (var i = 0; i < rows.length; i++) {
            table.append(rows[i]);
        }
    });

    function compare(index) {
        return function (a, b) {
            var valA = getCellValue(a, index), valB = getCellValue(b, index);
            return $.isNumeric(valA) && $.isNumeric(valB) ? valA - valB :
valA.localeCompare(valB);
        };
    }

    function getCellValue(row, index) { return $(row).children('td').eq(index).text(); }
});
```

Exercise 3.5 Form validation

Html File:

```html
<!DOCTYPE html>
<html lang="en">
<head>
    <meta charset="UTF-8">
    <meta name="viewport" content="width=device-width, initial-scale=1.0">
    <title>Exercise 3.5</title>
    <style>
        /* CSS styles for form elements */
        body {
            font-family: Arial, sans-serif;
            background-color: #f4f4f4;
            padding: 20px;
        }

        form {
            max-width: 400px;
            margin: 0 auto;
            background-color: #fff;
            padding: 20px;
            border-radius: 8px;
            box-shadow: 0 0 10px rgba(0, 0, 0, 0.1);
        }

        input[type="text"], input[type="email"], input[type="password"] {
            margin-bottom: 15px;
            padding: 10px;
            width: calc(100% - 20px);
            border: 1px solid #ccc;
            border-radius: 5px;
```

```css
        font-size: 16px;
    }

    .error {
        color: #ff0000;
        font-size: 14px;
        margin-bottom: 10px;
    }

    button[type="submit"] {
        background-color: #4caf50;
        color: #fff;
        padding: 10px 20px;
        border: none;
        border-radius: 5px;
        cursor: pointer;
        font-size: 16px;
    }

    button[type="submit"]:hover {
        background-color: #45a049;
    }
    </style>
</head>
<body>
    <form id="myForm">
        <input type="text" id="name" placeholder="Name">
        <span class="error" id="nameError"></span><br> <!-- Error message container -->
        <input type="email" id="email" placeholder="Email">
        <span class="error" id="emailError"></span><br> <!-- Error message container -->
        <input type="password" id="password" placeholder="Password">
        <span class="error" id="passwordError"></span><br> <!-- Error message container -->
```

```html
    <button type="submit">Submit</button>
  </form>
  <script src="https://code.jquery.com/jquery-3.6.0.min.js"></script>
  <script src="Form_validation.js"></script>
</body>
</html>
```

JavaScript File (Form_validation.js):

```javascript
$(document).ready(function () {
    // Form submission handler
    $('#myForm').submit(function (e) {
        e.preventDefault(); // Prevent default form submission

        // Retrieve form input values
        var name = $('#name').val();
        var email = $('#email').val();
        var password = $('#password').val();

        // Validation
        if (name.trim() === '') {
            $('#nameError').text('Name is required'); // Display error message
            return;
        } else {
            $('#nameError').text(''); // Clear error message
        }

        if (!/^\S+@\S+\.\S+$/.test(email)) {
            $('#emailError').text('Invalid email format'); // Display error message
            return;
        } else {
            $('#emailError').text(''); // Clear error message
        }
```

```javascript
        if (password.length < 8) {
            $('#passwordError').text('Password must be at least 8 characters'); // Display error
message
            return;
        } else {
            $('#passwordError').text(''); // Clear error message
        }


        // If all validations pass, submit the form
        alert('Form submitted successfully!');
    });
});
```

Exercise 3.6 Navbar

Html File:

```html
<!DOCTYPE html>
<html lang="en">
<head>
  <meta charset="UTF-8">
  <meta name="viewport" content="width=device-width, initial-scale=1.0">
  <title>Exercise 3.6</title>
  <style>
    /* Basic styling for navbar */
    body {
        font-family: Arial, sans-serif;
        margin: 0;
        padding: 0;
        background-color: #f4f4f4; /* Background color */
    }

    header {
        background-color: #ff4081; /* Pink */
```

```css
    color: #fff;
    padding: 10px 0;
}

.navbar {
    list-style-type: none;
    margin: 0;
    padding: 0;
    text-align: center;
}

    .navbar li {
        display: inline-block;
        margin: 0 15px;
    }

        .navbar li a {
            color: #fff;
            text-decoration: none;
            font-size: 18px;
            padding: 10px;
            transition: background-color 0.3s;
        }

            .navbar li a:hover {
                background-color: #aa00ff; /* Dark pink */
            }

/* Dropdown menu */
.dropdown {
    position: relative;
}
```

```css
.dropdown-content {
    display: none;
    position: absolute;
    background-color: #64b5f6; /* Blue */
    min-width: 200px;
    z-index: 1;
    padding: 10px 0;
    left: 0;
}

.dropdown-content li {
    display: block;
    text-align: left;
}

.dropdown-content li a {
    display: block;
    padding: 10px 20px;
    color: #fff;
    text-decoration: none;
    transition: background-color 0.3s;
}

.dropdown-content li a:hover {
    background-color: #2196f3; /* Light blue */
}

.dropdown:hover .dropdown-content {
    display: block;
}
```

```css
/* Submenu for Electronics */
.sub-menu {
    display: none;
    position: absolute;
    background-color: #00bcd4; /* Cyan */
    min-width: 200px;
    z-index: 1;
    top: 0;
    left: 100%;
}

    .sub-menu li {
        display: block;
        text-align: left;
    }

        .sub-menu li a {
            display: block;
            padding: 10px 20px;
            color: #fff;
            text-decoration: none;
            transition: background-color 0.3s;
        }

            .sub-menu li a:hover {
                background-color: #0097a7; /* Dark cyan */
            }

.dropdown-content li:hover .sub-menu {
    display: block;
}
```

```css
.dropdown-content li:hover .sub-menu li {
    display: block;
}

/* Third level submenu */
.sub-sub-menu {
    display: none;
    position: absolute;
    background-color: #4caf50; /* Green */
    min-width: 200px;
    z-index: 1;
    top: 0;
    left: 100%;
}

    .sub-sub-menu li {
        display: block;
        text-align: left;
    }

        .sub-sub-menu li a {
            display: block;
            padding: 10px 20px;
            color: #fff;
            text-decoration: none;
            transition: background-color 0.3s;
        }

        .sub-sub-menu li a:hover {
            background-color: #087f23; /* Dark green */
        }
```

```css
.sub-menu li:hover .sub-sub-menu {
    display: block;
}

.sub-menu li:hover .sub-sub-menu li {
    display: block;
}

.content {
    padding: 20px;
    background-color: #fff; /* Content background color */
    border-radius: 8px; /* Content border radius */
    box-shadow: 0 2px 4px rgba(0, 0, 0, 0.1); /* Content box shadow */
}

.content h2 {
    color: #333;
}

.content p {
    color: #666;
    line-height: 1.6;
}
    </style>
</head>
<body>
    <header>
        <nav>
            <!-- Navigation bar -->
            <ul class="navbar">
                <li><a href="#" class="nav-link" data-page="home">Home</a></li>
                <li class="dropdown">
```

```html
<a href="#" class="nav-link">Products</a>
<!-- Dropdown content -->
<ul class="dropdown-content">
  <li>
    <!-- Electronics category with submenu -->
    <a href="#" class="nav-link" data-page="electronics">Electronics</a>
    <!-- Submenu for Electronics -->
    <ul class="sub-menu">
      <li>
        <a href="#" class="nav-link" data-page="phones">Phones</a>
        <!-- Sub-submenu for Phones -->
        <ul class="sub-sub-menu">
          <li><a href="#" class="nav-link" data-page="iphone">iPhone</a></li>
          <li><a href="#" class="nav-link" data-page="samsung">Samsung</a></li>
          <li><a href="#" class="nav-link" data-page="google">Google Pixel</a></li>
        </ul>
      </li>
      <li><a href="#" class="nav-link" data-page="laptops">Laptops</a></li>
      <li><a href="#" class="nav-link" data-page="tablets">Tablets</a></li>
    </ul>
  </li>
  <li><a href="#" class="nav-link" data-page="clothing">Clothing</a></li>
  <li><a href="#" class="nav-link" data-page="books">Books</a></li>
</ul>
</li>
<li><a href="#" class="nav-link" data-page="about">About</a></li>
<li><a href="#" class="nav-link" data-page="contact">Contact</a></li>
</ul>
</nav>
```

```html
    </header>

    <main class="content">
        <!-- Content will be loaded dynamically here -->
    </main>


    <script src="https://code.jquery.com/jquery-3.6.0.min.js"></script>
    <script src="Navbar.js"></script>
</body>
</html>
```

JavaScript File (Navbar.js):

```javascript
$(document).ready(function () {
    // Function to load page content dynamically
    function loadPage(page) {
        var content;
        switch (page) {
            case "home":
                content = `
                    <h2>Welcome to Our Product Store!</h2>
                    <p>This is the Home page content. Feel free to explore our products and
contact us for any inquiries.</p>
                    `;
                break;
            case "electronics":
                content = `
                    <h2>Electronics</h2>
                    <p>Explore our range of electronic products...</p>
                    <ul>
                        <li>Smartphones</li>
                        <li>Laptops</li>
```

```
            <li>Tablets</li>
        </ul>
    `;
    break;
case "phones":
    content = `
        <h2>Phones</h2>
        <p>Discover our latest smartphone collection...</p>
    `;
    break;
case "laptops":
    content = `
        <h2>Laptops</h2>
        <p>Explore our powerful laptops...</p>
    `;
    break;
case "tablets":
    content = `
        <h2>Tablets</h2>
        <p>Check out our versatile tablet devices...</p>
    `;
    break;
case "clothing":
    content = `
        <h2>Clothing</h2>
        <p>Discover our latest clothing collection...</p>
        <ul>
            <li>T-shirts</li>
            <li>Jeans</li>
            <li>Dresses</li>
        </ul>
    `;
```

```
        break;
    case "books":
        content = `
            <h2>Books</h2>
            <p>Find your next favorite book...</p>
            <ul>
                <li>Fiction</li>
                <li>Non-fiction</li>
                <li>Sci-Fi</li>
            </ul>
        `;
        break;
    case "about":
        content = `
            <h2>About Us</h2>
            <p>Learn more about our company...</p>
            <p>We are committed to providing high-quality products and excellent
customer service.</p>
        `;
        break;
    case "contact":
        content = `
            <h2>Contact Us</h2>
            <p>Feel free to reach out to us for any queries or feedback.</p>
            <p>Email: contact@example.com</p>
            <p>Phone: 163-486-7880</p>
        `;
        break;
    default:
        content = "<p>Error: Page not found.</p>";
}
$(".content").html(content);
```

```
      }

      // Initial page load
      loadPage("home");

      // Event listener for navbar links
      $(".nav-link").click(function (event) {
        event.preventDefault();
        var page = $(this).data("page");
        loadPage(page);
      });
    });
```

Exercise 3.7 Authentication Page
Html File:

```
<!DOCTYPE html>
<html lang="en">
<head>
  <meta charset="UTF-8">
  <meta name="viewport" content="width=device-width, initial-scale=1.0">
  <title>Exercise 3.7</title>
  <style>
    .container {
      width: 300px;
      margin: 100px auto;
      text-align: center;
    }

    .form-group {
      margin-bottom: 20px;
    }
```

```css
        label {
            display: block;
            margin-bottom: 5px;
        }

        input[type="text"],
        input[type="password"] {
            width: 100%;
            padding: 10px;
            margin-top: 5px;
            border-radius: 5px;
            border: 1px solid #ccc;
        }

        button {
            padding: 10px 20px;
            background-color: #007bff;
            color: #fff;
            border: none;
            border-radius: 5px;
            cursor: pointer;
        }

        button:hover {
            background-color: #0056b3;
        }
    </style>
</head>
<body>
    <div class="container">
        <h2>Authentication Page</h2>
```

```html
<form id="loginForm">
    <div class="form-group">
        <label for="username">Username:</label>
        <input type="text" id="username" name="username" required>
    </div>
    <div class="form-group">
        <label for="password">Password:</label>
        <input type="password" id="password" name="password" required>
    </div>
    <button type="submit">Login</button>
    <p id="error-msg"></p>
</form>
</div>
<script src="https://ajax.googleapis.com/ajax/libs/jquery/3.5.1/jquery.min.js"></script>
<script src="Authentication.js">    </script>
</body>
</html>
```

JavaScript File (Authentication.js):

```javascript
$(document).ready(function () {
    $('#loginForm').submit(function (event) {
        event.preventDefault();
        var username = $('#username').val();
        var password = $('#password').val();

        // Dummy authentication - replace this with actual authentication logic
        if (username === 'admin' && password === 'password') {
            // If authentication is successful, redirect or show success message
            alert('Login successful!');
            // Redirect to another page
            // window.location.href = 'dashboard.html';
        } else {
            // If authentication fails, display error message
```

```
                $('#error-msg').text('Invalid username or password. Please try again.');
            }
        });
    });
```

Exercise 3.8 Ajax Get Request

Html File:

```html
<!DOCTYPE html>
<html lang="en">
<head>
  <meta charset="UTF-8">
  <meta name="viewport" content="width=device-width, initial-scale=1.0">
  <title> Exercise 3.8</title>
</head>
<body>
  <input type="text" id="searchInput" placeholder="Enter search term">
  <button id="searchBtn">Search</button>
  <div id="searchResults"></div>
  <script src="https://code.jquery.com/jquery-3.6.0.min.js"></script>
  <script src="Get_request.js">    </script>
  <style>
    /* CSS styles for search results */
    .repo {
        margin-bottom: 20px;
        border: 1px solid #ccc;
        padding: 10px;
        border-radius: 5px;
        background-color: #f9f9f9;
    }

    .repo a {
        font-weight: bold;
        color: #0366d6;
```

```css
        text-decoration: none;
      }

    .description {
      margin-top: 5px;
      color: #666;
    }
  </style>
</body>
</html>
```

JavaScript File (Get_request.js):

```javascript
$(document).ready(function () {
    // Event listener for the search button click
    $('#searchBtn').click(function () {
        var searchTerm = $('#searchInput').val();

        // AJAX request to GitHub API
        $.ajax({
            url: 'https://api.github.com/search/repositories?q=' + searchTerm, // GitHub API URL
            method: 'GET',
            success: function (response) {
                // Clear previous search results
                $('#searchResults').empty();

                // Check if any results are found
                if (response.items.length > 0) {
                    // Loop through each repository and display relevant information
                    $.each(response.items, function (index, item) {
                        var repoName = item.full_name;
                        var repoURL = item.html_url;
                        var repoDescription = item.description || 'No description available';
```

```javascript
            // Create a div to display repository information
            var repoDiv = $('<div class="repo"></div>');

            // Add repository name as a link
            var repoLink = $('<a href="' + repoURL + '">' + repoName + '</a>');

            // Create a paragraph for repository description
            var descriptionPara = $('<p class="description">' + repoDescription +
'</p>');

            // Append link and description to the div
            repoDiv.append(repoLink, descriptionPara);

            // Append the div to the search results container
            $('#searchResults').append(repoDiv);
          });
        } else {
          // Display message if no results are found
          $('#searchResults').text('No repositories found');
        }
      },
      error: function () {
        // Display error message if AJAX request fails
        $('#searchResults').text('Error fetching data');
      }
    });
  });
});
```

Exercise 3.9 POST Request Example

Html File:

```html
<!DOCTYPE html>
```

```html
<html lang="en">
<head>
    <meta charset="UTF-8">
    <meta name="viewport" content="width=device-width, initial-scale=1.0">
    <title> Exercise 3.9 </title>
    <style>
        body {
            font-family: Arial, sans-serif;
            background-color: #f4f4f4;
            margin: 0;
            padding: 0;
        }

        .container {
            width: 400px;
            margin: 100px auto;
            background-color: #fff;
            padding: 20px;
            border-radius: 8px;
            box-shadow: 0px 0px 10px 0px rgba(0,0,0,0.1);
        }

        h2 {
            margin-top: 0;
            text-align: center;
            color: #333;
        }

        .form-group {
            margin-bottom: 20px;
        }
```

```css
label {
    display: block;
    margin-bottom: 5px;
    color: #666;
}

input[type="text"],
input[type="email"] {
    width: calc(100% - 12px);
    padding: 10px;
    margin-top: 5px;
    border-radius: 5px;
    border: 1px solid #ccc;
}

button {
    padding: 10px 20px;
    background-color: #007bff;
    color: #fff;
    border: none;
    border-radius: 5px;
    cursor: pointer;
    transition: background-color 0.3s ease;
}

    button:hover {
        background-color: #0056b3;
    }

#response {
    text-align: center;
    margin-top: 20px;
```

```html
        font-weight: bold;
      }
    </style>
  </head>
  <body>
    <div class="container">
      <h2>POST Request Example</h2>
      <form id="postForm">
        <div class="form-group">
          <label for="name">Name:</label>
          <input type="text" id="name" name="name" required>
        </div>
        <div class="form-group">
          <label for="email">Email:</label>
          <input type="email" id="email" name="email" required>
        </div>
        <button type="submit">Submit</button>
        <p id="response"></p>
      </form>
    </div>

    <script src="https://ajax.googleapis.com/ajax/libs/jquery/3.5.1/jquery.min.js"></script>
    <script src="Postdata.js">   </script>
  </body>
</html>
```

JavaScript File (Postdata.js):

```javascript
$(document).ready(function () {
    // When the form is submitted
    $('#postForm').submit(function (event) {
        // Prevent default form submission
        event.preventDefault();
```

```javascript
// Get the values from form fields
var name = $('#name').val();
var email = $('#email').val();

// Send a POST request using AJAX
$.ajax({
    // Specify request type
    type: 'POST',
    // URL to which the request is sent
    url: 'https://jsonplaceholder.typicode.com/posts',
    // Data to be sent to the server
    data: JSON.stringify({ name: name, email: email }),
    // Content type of the data being sent
    contentType: 'application/json',
    // Function to be called if the request succeeds
    success: function (response) {
        // Display success message
        $('#response').text('POST request successful!');
        // Log the response to the console
        console.log(response);
    },
    // Function to be called if the request fails
    error: function (xhr, status, error) {
        // Display error message
        $('#response').text('Error occurred while making the POST request.');
        // Log the error to the console
        console.error(error);
    }
    });
    });
});
```

Exercise 3.10 AJAX Data Visualization

Html File:

```html
<!DOCTYPE html>
<html lang="en">
<head>
   <meta charset="UTF-8">
   <meta name="viewport" content="width=device-width, initial-scale=1.0">
   <title> Exercise 3.10</title>
   <script src="https://ajax.googleapis.com/ajax/libs/jquery/3.5.1/jquery.min.js"></script>
   <script src="https://cdn.jsdelivr.net/npm/chart.js"></script>
</head>
<body>
   <div>
      <canvas id="weatherChart" width="800" height="400"></canvas>
   </div>
 <script src="WeatherChart.js">   </script>
</body>
</html>
```

JavaScript File (WeatherChart.js):

```javascript
    $(document).ready(function () {
      function generateDummyData() {
        var labels = [];
        var temperatures = [];

        // Generate dummy data for the past week
        for (var i = 6; i >= 0; i--) {
          var date = new Date();
          date.setDate(date.getDate() - i);
          labels.push(date.toDateString());
          // Generate random temperatures between 0 and 30 degrees Celsius
          temperatures.push(Math.floor(Math.random() * 31));
        }
```

```javascript
        return { labels: labels, temperatures: temperatures };
    }


    function createChart(labels, temperatures) {
        var ctx = document.getElementById('weatherChart').getContext('2d');
        var chart = new Chart(ctx, {
            type: 'line',
            data: {
                labels: labels,
                datasets: [{
                    label: 'Average Temperature (°C)',
                    data: temperatures,
                    backgroundColor: 'rgba(75, 192, 192, 0.2)',
                    borderColor: 'rgba(75, 192, 192, 1)',
                    borderWidth: 1
                }]
            }
        });
    }


    var dummyData = generateDummyData();
    createChart(dummyData.labels, dummyData.temperatures);
});
```

Exercise 3.11 Carousel Slider

Html File:

```html
<!DOCTYPE html>
<html lang="en">
<head>
  <meta charset="UTF-8">
  <meta name="viewport" content="width=device-width, initial-scale=1.0">
  <title> Exercise 3.11</title>
```

```
<style>
  body {
    margin: 0;
    font-family: Arial, sans-serif;
  }

  /* Carousel styling */
  .carousel {
    position: relative;
    width: 100%;
    max-width: 800px; /* Limiting the width of the carousel */
    margin: 0 auto; /* Centering the carousel */
    overflow: hidden;
  }

  .carousel-inner {
    display: flex;
    transition: transform 0.5s ease;
  }

  .carousel-item {
    flex: 0 0 100%;
    max-width: 100%;
    display: flex;
    justify-content: center;
  }

    .carousel-item img {
      max-width: 100%;
      height: auto;
    }
```

```css
/* Carousel control styling */
.carousel-control {
    position: absolute;
    top: 50%;
    transform: translateY(-50%);
    color: #fff;
    text-decoration: none;
    font-size: 2em;
    z-index: 999;
    background-color: rgba(0, 0, 0, 0.5);
    padding: 10px;
    border-radius: 50%;
    transition: background-color 0.3s ease;
}

.carousel-control:hover {
    background-color: rgba(0, 0, 0, 0.8);
}

.prev {
    left: 10px;
}

.next {
    right: 10px;
}
</style>
</head>
<body>
    <div class="carousel">
        <div class="carousel-inner">
            <div class="carousel-item active">
```

```html
        <img src="example1.jpg" alt="Slide 1">
      </div>
      <div class="carousel-item">
        <img src="example2.jpg" alt="Slide 2">
      </div>
      <div class="carousel-item">
        <img src="example3.jpg" alt="Slide 3">
      </div>
    </div>
    <a class="carousel-control prev" href="#">&laquo;</a>
    <a class="carousel-control next" href="#">&raquo;</a>
  </div>


  <script src="https://code.jquery.com/jquery-3.6.0.min.js"></script>
  <script src="carousel.js"> </script>
</body>
</html>
```

JavaScript File (carousel.js):

```javascript
$(document).ready(function () {
    var currentIndex = 0; // Index of the current slide
    var items = $('.carousel-item'); // All carousel items
    var totalItems = items.length; // Total number of items in the carousel
    var slideInterval = 3000; // Interval between slides in milliseconds

    // Function to go to a specific slide by its index
    function goToIndex(index) {
      if (index < 0) {
        index = totalItems - 1;
      } else if (index >= totalItems) {
        index = 0;
      }
      $('.carousel-inner').css('transform', 'translateX(-' + (index * 100) + '%)');
```

```javascript
        currentIndex = index;
    }


    // Function to automatically go to the next slide
    function slideNext() {
        goToIndex(currentIndex + 1);
    }


    // Start automatic sliding
    var slideTimer = setInterval(slideNext, slideInterval);


    // Pause sliding on hover and resume on mouseout
    $('.carousel-control').hover(
        function () {
            clearInterval(slideTimer);
        },
        function () {
            slideTimer = setInterval(slideNext, slideInterval);
        }
    );


    // Previous slide button click event
    $('.prev').click(function () {
        goToIndex(currentIndex - 1);
    });


    // Next slide button click event
    $('.next').click(function () {
        goToIndex(currentIndex + 1);
    });
});
```

Chapter 4

Object-Oriented Programming

4 Object-Oriented Programming

4.1 Exercises

Exercise 4.1 Blog Post Management

Create a class `BlogPost` with properties `title`, `content`, `author`, and `date`. Add methods to create, edit, and delete blog posts. Store the blog posts in an array and implement a method to list all posts (Example: Figure 4.1).

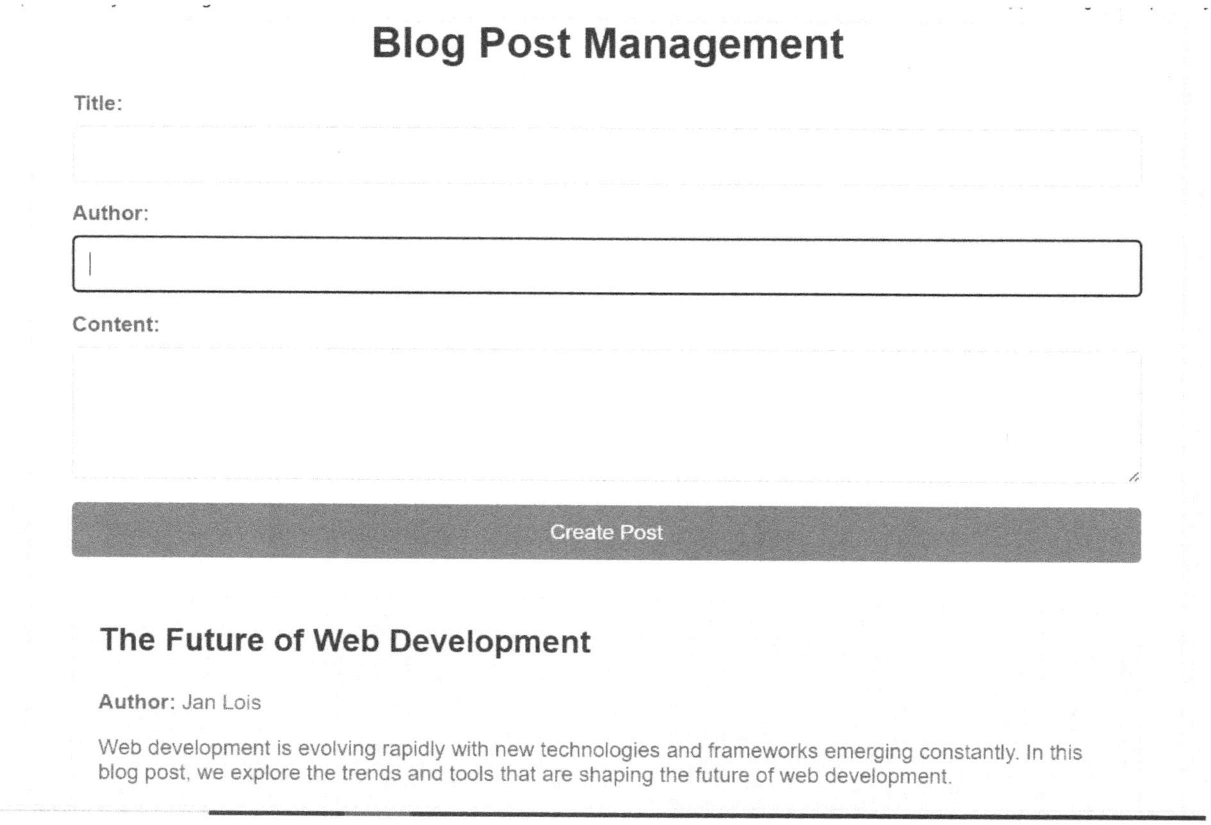

Blog Post Management

Title:

Author:

Content:

Create Post

The Future of Web Development

Author: Jan Lois

Web development is evolving rapidly with new technologies and frameworks emerging constantly. In this blog post, we explore the trends and tools that are shaping the future of web development.

Figure 4.1 Blog Post Management

Exercise 4.2: User Authentication System

Create classes `User` and `Auth`. The `User` class should have properties `username`, `password`, and `email`. The `Auth` class should handle user registration and login, including methods `register()` and `login()`. Implement basic validation and storage of users in an in-memory array (Example: Figure 4.2).

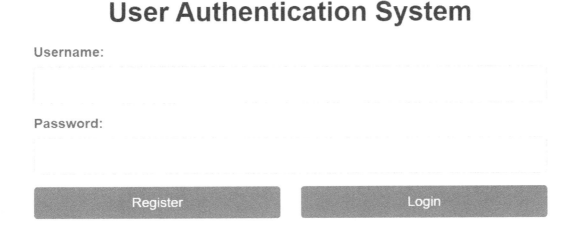

Figure 4.2 User Authentication System

Exercise 4.3 Shopping Cart (with local storage)

Create classes `Product`, `CartItem`, and `ShoppingCart`. The `Product` class should include properties like `id`, `name`, and `price`. The `CartItem` class should include `product` and `quantity`. The `ShoppingCart` class should manage adding, removing, and listing items in the cart, as well as calculating the total price. The application should contain two pages (Example: Figure 4.3(a), and Figure 4.3 (b)):

1. **Product Management Page (`products.html`):**
   - This page allows the user to add new products and display the list of added products.
   - Products are stored in the browser's local storage to persist between sessions.
   - Create a button to navigate to the shopping cart page.

2. **Cart Management Page (`cart.html`):**
   - This page allows the user to add products to the cart, view the cart items, update quantities, and remove items.

- Products available for selection are fetched from the local storage.
- Cart items are stored in local storage to persist between sessions.
- Create a button to navigate back to the products management page.

Product Management

Add Product

Product Name:

Product Price:

Add Product

Products

Orange - $7.00   Remove

Lemon - $7.00   Remove

Go to Cart

Figure 4.3(a) Product Management page

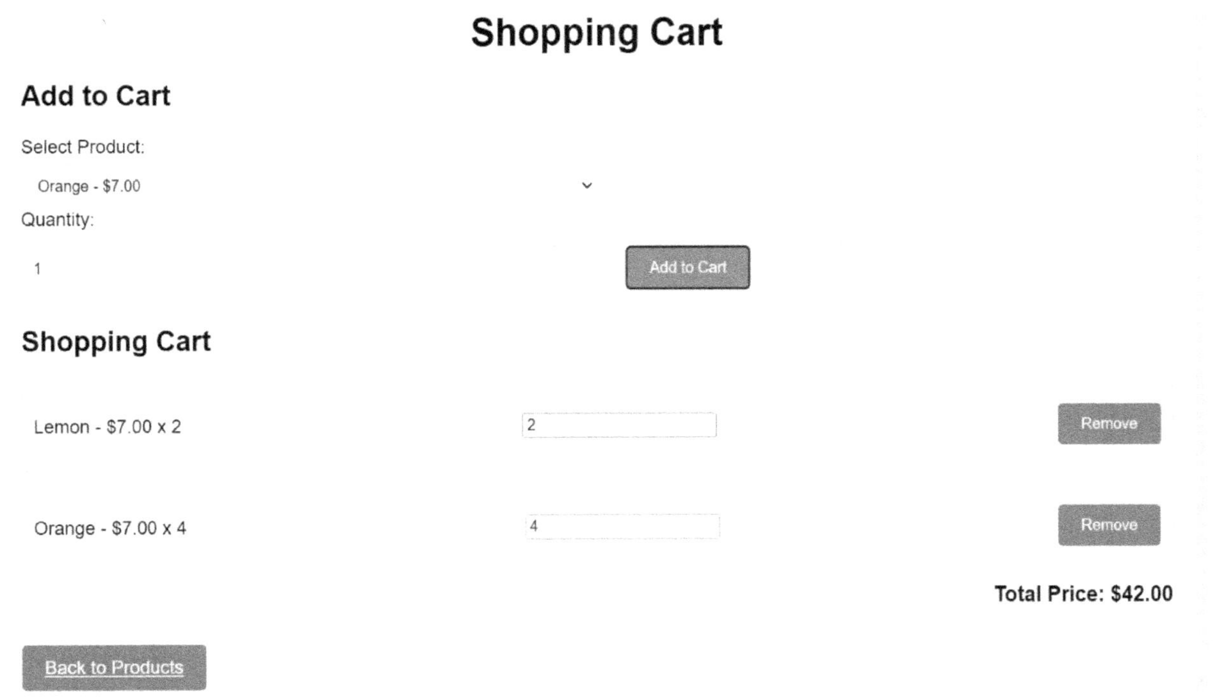

Shopping Cart

Add to Cart

Select Product:

Orange - $7.00   ⌄

Quantity:

1   [Add to Cart]

Shopping Cart

Lemon - $7.00 x 2 | 2 | [Remove]

Orange - $7.00 x 4 | 4 | [Remove]

Total Price: $42.00

[Back to Products]

Figure 4.3(b) Shopping Cart page

Exercise 4.4 Messaging System (with local storage)

Create classes `Message` and `UserInbox`. The `Message` class should have properties `sender`, `recipient`, `content`, and `timestamp`. The `UserInbox` class should handle sending and receiving messages, as well as listing messages for a specific user (Example: Figure 4.4(a), and figure 4.4(b)). The messaging system should be with user authentication and use local storage to handle sent and received messages. The solution includes a predefined set of users.

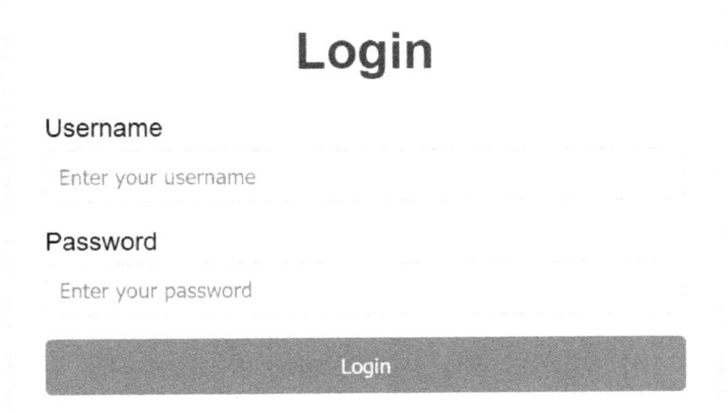

Login

Username

Enter your username

Password

Enter your password

[Login]

Figure 4.4(a) Authentication Page

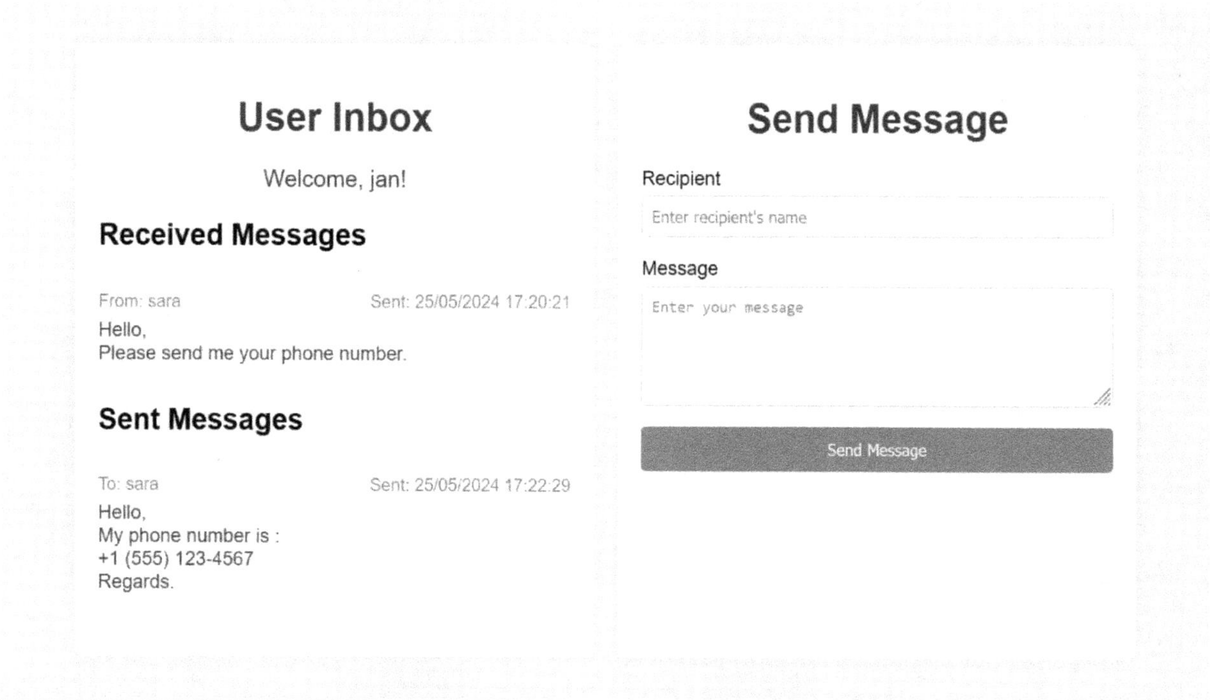

User Inbox

Welcome, jan!

Received Messages

From: sara   Sent: 25/05/2024 17:20:21

Hello,
Please send me your phone number.

Sent Messages

To: sara   Sent: 25/05/2024 17:22:29

Hello,
My phone number is :
+1 (555) 123-4567
Regards.

Send Message

Recipient

Enter recipient's name

Message

Enter your message

Send Message

Figure 4.4(b) User Inbox Page

4.2 Solutions

Exercise 4.1

Html File :

```html
<!DOCTYPE html>
<html lang="en">
<head>
  <meta charset="UTF-8">
  <meta name="viewport" content="width=device-width, initial-scale=1.0">
  <title>Blog Post Management</title>
  <style>

    body {
        font-family: 'Helvetica Neue', Helvetica, Arial, sans-serif;
        background-color: #f7f9fc;
        margin: 0;
        padding: 0;
        color: #333;
    }

    .container {
        max-width: 800px;
        margin: 50px auto;
        background-color: #fff;
        padding: 30px;
        border-radius: 8px;
        box-shadow: 0 4px 8px rgba(0, 0, 0, 0.1);
    }

    h2 {
```

```css
    text-align: center;
    color: #333;
    font-size: 2em;
    margin-bottom: 20px;
}

label {
    display: block;
    margin-bottom: 8px;
    font-weight: bold;
    color: #555;
}

input[type="text"],
textarea {
    width: 100%;
    padding: 12px;
    margin-bottom: 15px;
    border: 1px solid #ccc;
    border-radius: 4px;
    box-sizing: border-box;
    font-size: 1em;
}

input[type="submit"] {
    width: 100%;
    padding: 12px;
    background-color: #007bff;
    color: #fff;
    border: none;
    border-radius: 4px;
    cursor: pointer;
```

```css
    font-size: 1em;
    transition: background-color 0.3s;
}

    input[type="submit"]:hover {
        background-color: #0056b3;
    }

.blog-posts {
    margin-top: 30px;
}

.blog-post {
    border: 1px solid #e1e4e8;
    border-radius: 8px;
    padding: 20px;
    margin-bottom: 20px;
    background-color: #f7f9fc;
}

    .blog-post h3 {
        margin-top: 0;
        font-size: 1.5em;
        color: #333;
    }

    .blog-post p {
        margin-bottom: 10px;
        color: #555;
    }

    .blog-post .date {
```

```
            color: #999;
            font-size: 0.9em;
        }
    </style>
</head>
<body>
    <div class="container">
        <h2>Blog Post Management</h2>
        <form id="blogPostForm">
            <label for="title">Title:</label>
            <input type="text" id="title" name="title" required>
            <label for="author">Author:</label>
            <input type="text" id="author" name="author" required>
            <label for="content">Content:</label>
            <textarea id="content" name="content" rows="5" required></textarea>
            <input type="submit" value="Create Post">
        </form>
        <div class="blog-posts" id="blogPosts">
            <!-- Blog posts will be displayed here -->
        </div>
    </div>

    <script src="blog.js"> </script>
</body>
</html>
```

JavaScript File (blog.js):

```
// Define the BlogPost class
class BlogPost {
    constructor(title, content, author, date) {
        this.title = title;
        this.content = content;
```

```javascript
    this.author = author;
    this.date = date || new Date().toLocaleDateString();
  }
}


// Define the Blog class to manage blog posts
class Blog {
  constructor() {
    // Initialize blog posts array
    this.posts = [];
  }

  // Method to create a new blog post
  createPost(post) {
    this.posts.push(post);
  }

  // Method to display all blog posts
  displayPosts() {
    const blogPostsElement = document.getElementById("blogPosts");
    blogPostsElement.innerHTML = ""; // Clear existing posts

    this.posts.forEach(post => {
      const postElement = document.createElement("div");
      postElement.classList.add("blog-post");
      postElement.innerHTML = `
        <h3>${post.title}</h3>
        <p><strong>Author:</strong> ${post.author}</p>
        <p>${post.content}</p>
        <p class="date"><em>${post.date}</em></p>
      `;
      blogPostsElement.appendChild(postElement);
```

```
<meta charset="UTF-8">
<meta name="viewport" content="width=device-width, initial-scale=1.0">
<title>User Authentication System</title>
<style>

    body {
        font-family: 'Helvetica Neue', Helvetica, Arial, sans-serif;
        background-color: #f7f9fc;
        margin: 0;
        padding: 20px;
        color: #333;
    }

    .container {
        max-width: 600px;
        margin: 50px auto;
        background-color: #fff;
        padding: 30px;
        border-radius: 8px;
        box-shadow: 0 4px 8px rgba(0, 0, 0, 0.1);
    }

    h2 {
        text-align: center;
        color: #333;
        font-size: 2em;
        margin-bottom: 20px;
    }

    label {
        display: block;
        margin-bottom: 8px;
```

```css
        font-weight: bold;
        color: #555;
    }

input[type="text"], input[type="password"], input[type="email"] {
        width: 100%;
        padding: 12px;
        margin-bottom: 15px;
        border: 1px solid #ccc;
        border-radius: 4px;
        box-sizing: border-box;
        font-size: 1em;
    }

.btn-container {
        display: flex;
        justify-content: space-between;
    }

    .btn-container button {
            width: 48%;
            padding: 10px; /* Smaller button size */
            background-color: #007bff;
            color: #fff;
            border: none;
            border-radius: 4px;
            cursor: pointer;
            font-size: 1em;
            transition: background-color 0.3s;
        }

        .btn-container button:hover {
```

```
        background-color: #0056b3;
    }


    .auth-results {
      margin-top: 30px;
    }


    .auth-results p {
      color: #555;
    }
    </style>
</head>
<body>
  <div class="container">
    <h2>User Authentication System</h2>
    <form id="authForm">
      <label for="username">Username:</label>
      <input type="text" id="username" name="username" required>
      <label for="password">Password:</label>
      <input type="password" id="password" name="password" required>
      <div id="emailContainer" style="display: none;">
        <label for="email">Email:</label>
        <input type="email" id="email" name="email">
      </div>
      <div class="btn-container">
        <button type="button" id="registerBtn">Register</button>
        <button type="button" id="loginBtn">Login</button>
      </div>
    </form>
    <div class="auth-results" id="authResults">
      <!-- Authentication results will be displayed here -->
    </div>
```

```html
    </div>

    <script src="Auth.js">    </script>
</body>
</html>
```

JavaScript File (Auth.js):

```javascript
// Define the User class
class User {
    // Constructor to initialize user properties
    constructor(username, password, email) {
        this.username = username;
        this.password = password;
        this.email = email;
    }
}

// Define the Auth class
class Auth {
    // Constructor to initialize the users array
    constructor() {
        this.users = [];
    }

    // Method to register a new user
    register(user) {
        // Check if the user already exists in the array
        const userExists = this.users.some(u => u.username === user.username);
        if (userExists) {
            return "User already exists!";
        }
        // Add the new user to the users array
        this.users.push(user);
```

```javascript
            return "User registered successfully!";
        }


    // Method to login a user
    login(username, password) {
        // Check if the username and password match any user in the array
        const user = this.users.find(u => u.username === username && u.password ===
password);
        // Return appropriate message based on the result
        return user ? "Login successful!" : "Invalid username or password!";
        }
    }


// Create an instance of Auth class
const auth = new Auth();


// Function to handle registration
function handleRegister(event) {
    event.preventDefault(); // Prevent default form submission


    // Get form inputs
    const username = document.getElementById("username").value;
    const password = document.getElementById("password").value;
    const email = document.getElementById("email").value;


    // Create a new user object and register the user
    const newUser = new User(username, password, email);
    const result = auth.register(newUser);


    // Display the result of the registration
    const authResultsElement = document.getElementById("authResults");
    authResultsElement.innerHTML = `<p>${result}</p>`;
```

```javascript
    // Clear the form
    document.getElementById("authForm").reset();
    document.getElementById("emailContainer").style.display = "none";
}


// Function to handle login
function handleLogin(event) {
    event.preventDefault(); // Prevent default form submission

    // Get form inputs
    const username = document.getElementById("username").value;
    const password = document.getElementById("password").value;

    // Attempt to login the user
    const result = auth.login(username, password);

    // Display the result of the login attempt
    const authResultsElement = document.getElementById("authResults");
    authResultsElement.innerHTML = `<p>${result}</p>`;

    // Clear the form
    document.getElementById("authForm").reset();
}


// Event listener for the register button
document.getElementById("registerBtn").addEventListener("click", function () {
    // Show the email input field
    document.getElementById("emailContainer").style.display = "block";
    // Set the form submission handler to handleRegister
    document.getElementById("authForm").onsubmit = handleRegister;
});
```

```javascript
// Event listener for the login button
document.getElementById("loginBtn").addEventListener("click", function () {
    // Hide the email input field
    document.getElementById("emailContainer").style.display = "none";
    // Set the form submission handler to handleLogin
    document.getElementById("authForm").onsubmit = handleLogin;
});
```

Exercise 4.3

Html File (products.html):

```html
<!DOCTYPE html>
<html lang="en">
<head>
    <meta charset="UTF-8">
    <meta name="viewport" content="width=device-width, initial-scale=1.0">
    <title>Product Management</title>
    <style>
        /* Basic styles for the page */
        body {
            font-family: Arial, sans-serif;
            background-color: #f0f0f0;
            margin: 0;
            padding: 0;
        }

        /* Container for the main content */
        .container {
            width: 80%;
            margin: 20px auto;
            background-color: #fff;
            padding: 20px;
```

```css
    border-radius: 8px;
    box-shadow: 0 0 10px rgba(0, 0, 0, 0.1);
}

/* Heading styles */
h1 {
    text-align: center;
}

.form-group {
    margin-bottom: 15px;
}

    .form-group label {
        display: block;
        margin-bottom: 5px;
    }

    .form-group input {
        width: 50%;
        padding: 10px;
        border: 1px solid #ddd;
        border-radius: 4px;
    }

/* Button styles */
.btn {
    display: inline-block;
    padding: 10px 20px;
    margin: 10px 0;
    border: none;
    border-radius: 4px;
```

```css
      cursor: pointer;
    }

    .btn-primary {
      background-color: #007bff;
      color: #fff;
    }

    .btn-danger {
      background-color: #dc3545;
      color: #fff;
    }

    /* Product list styles */
    .product-list {
      margin: 20px 0;
    }

    .product-item {
      display: flex;
      justify-content: space-between;
      align-items: center;
      padding: 10px;
      margin-bottom: 10px;
      border: 1px solid #ddd;
      border-radius: 4px;
    }
  </style>
</head>
<body>
  <div class="container">
    <h1>Product Management</h1>
```

```html
<div id="productForm" class="form-group">
  <h2>Add Product</h2>
  <!-- Input field for product name -->
  <label for="productName">Product Name:</label>
  <input type="text" id="productName">
  <!-- Input field for product price -->
  <label for="productPrice">Product Price:</label>
  <input type="number" id="productPrice" step="0.01">
  <!-- Button to add the product -->
  <button id="addProductBtn" class="btn btn-primary">Add Product</button>
</div>
<div class="product-list">
  <h2>Products</h2>
  <!-- Container to display the list of products -->
  <div id="productContainer"></div>
</div>
<!-- Link to go to the cart page -->
<a href="cart.html" class="btn btn-primary">Go to Cart</a>
</div>


<script>
<script src="products.js"> </script>
</body>
</html>
```

JavaScript File (products.js) :

```javascript
// Class to represent a Product
class Product {
  // Static property to keep track of the next ID
  static nextId = 1;
  constructor(name, price) {
    this.id = Product.nextId++; // Assign and increment the ID
    this.name = name; // Set the product name
```

```javascript
    this.price = parseFloat(price); // Set the product price
  }
}


// Array to store products
const products = [];


// Function to handle adding a new product
function handleAddProduct(event) {
  event.preventDefault(); // Prevent form submission
  const name = document.getElementById("productName").value; // Get product name
from input
  const price = document.getElementById("productPrice").value; // Get product price
from input
  if (name && price) { // Ensure both fields are filled
    const newProduct = new Product(name, price); // Create a new product instance
    products.push(newProduct); // Add the new product to the array
    updateProductList(); // Update the displayed product list
    document.getElementById("productName").value = ''; // Clear the name input field
    document.getElementById("productPrice").value = ''; // Clear the price input field
    localStorage.setItem('products', JSON.stringify(products)); // Save the updated
products to local storage
  }
}


// Function to update the displayed product list
function updateProductList() {
  const productContainer = document.getElementById("productContainer"); // Get the
container element
  productContainer.innerHTML = ''; // Clear the container
  products.forEach(product => {
    // Create a new div element for each product
```

```javascript
        const productItem = document.createElement("div");
        productItem.className = 'product-item'; // Add the product-item class
        productItem.innerHTML = `
            <span>${product.name} - $${product.price.toFixed(2)}</span>
            <button class="btn btn-danger"
onclick="removeProduct(${product.id})">Remove</button>
            `;
        productContainer.appendChild(productItem); // Append the product div to the
container
    });
}


    // Function to remove a product by ID
    function removeProduct(productId) {
        const productIndex = products.findIndex(product => product.id === productId); //
Find the product index
        if (productIndex !== -1) { // If the product exists
            products.splice(productIndex, 1); // Remove the product from the array
            updateProductList(); // Update the displayed product list
            localStorage.setItem('products', JSON.stringify(products)); // Save the updated
products to local storage
        }
    }


    // Add event listener to the add product button
    document.getElementById("addProductBtn").addEventListener("click",
handleAddProduct);


    // Load products from local storage when the page loads
    document.addEventListener("DOMContentLoaded", () => {
        const savedProducts = JSON.parse(localStorage.getItem('products')); // Get saved
products from local storage
```

```javascript
    if (savedProducts) {
        savedProducts.forEach(productData => {
            const product = new Product(productData.name, productData.price); // Create
product instances from saved data
            product.id = productData.id; // Restore the product ID
            Product.nextId = Math.max(Product.nextId, product.id + 1); // Ensure the next ID
is correct
            products.push(product); // Add the product to the array
        });
        updateProductList(); // Update the displayed product list
    }
});
```

Html file (cart.html):

```html
<!DOCTYPE html>
<html lang="en">
<head>
    <meta charset="UTF-8">
    <meta name="viewport" content="width=device-width, initial-scale=1.0">
    <title>Shopping Cart</title>
    <style>
        /* Basic styling for the page */
        body {
            font-family: Arial, sans-serif;
            background-color: #f0f0f0;
            margin: 0;
            padding: 0;
        }

        /* Container for the main content */
        .container {
            width: 80%;
            margin: 20px auto;
```

```css
    background-color: #fff;
    padding: 20px;
    border-radius: 8px;
    box-shadow: 0 0 10px rgba(0, 0, 0, 0.1);
}

/* Heading styles */
h1 {
    text-align: center;
}

.form-group {
    margin-bottom: 15px;
}

    .form-group label {
        display: block;
        margin-bottom: 5px;
    }

    .form-group select, .form-group input {
        width: 50%;
        padding: 10px;
        border: 1px solid #ddd;
        border-radius: 4px;
    }

/* Button styles */
.btn {
    display: inline-block;
    padding: 10px 20px;
    margin: 10px 0;
```

```css
  border: none;
  border-radius: 4px;
  cursor: pointer;
}

.btn-primary {
  background-color: #007bff;
  color: #fff;
}

.btn-secondary {
  background-color: #6c757d;
  color: #fff;
}

.btn-danger {
  background-color: #dc3545;
  color: #fff;
}

/* Cart list styles */
.cart-list {
  margin: 20px 0;
}

.cart-item {
  display: flex;
  justify-content: space-between;
  align-items: center;
  padding: 10px;
  margin-bottom: 10px;
  border: 1px solid #ddd;
```

```
        border-radius: 4px;
      }


    .total-price {
        text-align: right;
        font-size: 18px;
        font-weight: bold;
      }
    </style>
  </head>
  <body>
    <div class="container">
      <h1>Shopping Cart</h1>
      <div id="cartForm" class="form-group">
        <h2>Add to Cart</h2>
        <!-- Dropdown for selecting a product -->
        <label for="productSelect">Select Product:</label>
        <select id="productSelect"></select>
        <!-- Input for specifying the quantity -->
        <label for="productQuantity">Quantity:</label>
        <input type="number" id="productQuantity" value="1" min="1">
        <!-- Button to add the product to the cart -->
        <button id="addToCartBtn" class="btn btn-primary">Add to Cart</button>
      </div>
      <div class="cart-list">
        <h2>Shopping Cart</h2>
        <!-- Container to display the cart items -->
        <div id="cartContainer"></div>
        <!-- Display the total price of items in the cart -->
        <div id="totalPrice" class="total-price">Total Price: $0.00</div>
      </div>
      <!-- Link to navigate back to the products page -->
```

```html
        <a href="products.html" class="btn btn-secondary">Back to Products</a>
    </div>

    <script src="cart.js"> </script>
</body>
</html>
```

JavaScript File (cart.js):

```javascript
// Class representing an item in the cart
class CartItem {
    constructor(product, quantity) {
        this.product = product; // Product object
        this.quantity = parseInt(quantity); // Quantity of the product
    }
}


// Class representing the shopping cart
class ShoppingCart {
    constructor() {
        this.items = []; // Array to store cart items
    }


    // Add a new item to the cart
    addItem(cartItem) {
        const existingItem = this.items.find(item => item.product.id ===
cartItem.product.id);
        if (existingItem) {
            existingItem.quantity += cartItem.quantity; // Update quantity if item already
exists
        } else {
            this.items.push(cartItem); // Add new item to the cart
        }
    }
```

```javascript
// Remove an item from the cart by product ID
removeItem(productId) {
    this.items = this.items.filter(item => item.product.id !== productId);
}


// Update the quantity of a cart item by product ID
updateQuantity(productId, quantity) {
    const item = this.items.find(item => item.product.id === productId);
    if (item) {
        item.quantity = quantity; // Update the quantity
        if (item.quantity <= 0) {
            this.removeItem(productId); // Remove item if quantity is zero or less
        }
    }
}


// Calculate the total price of items in the cart
calculateTotal() {
    return this.items.reduce((total, item) => total + item.product.price * item.quantity,
0);
}


// Get the list of items in the cart
getItems() {
    return this.items;
    }
}


const shoppingCart = new ShoppingCart(); // Create a new shopping cart instance
const products = JSON.parse(localStorage.getItem('products')) || []; // Load products
from local storage
```

```javascript
// Function to update the product selection dropdown
function updateProductSelection() {
    const productSelect = document.getElementById("productSelect");
    productSelect.innerHTML = ''; // Clear the dropdown
    products.forEach(product => {
        const option = document.createElement("option");
        option.value = product.id; // Set the option value to the product ID
        option.textContent = `${product.name} - $${product.price.toFixed(2)}`; // Set the
option text
        productSelect.appendChild(option); // Add the option to the dropdown
    });
}


// Function to handle adding an item to the cart
function handleAddToCart(event) {
    event.preventDefault(); // Prevent form submission
    const productId = parseInt(document.getElementById("productSelect").value); // Get
selected product ID
    const quantity = parseInt(document.getElementById("productQuantity").value); // Get
quantity
    const selectedProduct = products.find(product => product.id === productId); // Find
the product by ID
    if (selectedProduct && quantity > 0) {
        const cartItem = new CartItem(selectedProduct, quantity); // Create a new cart item
        shoppingCart.addItem(cartItem); // Add the item to the cart
        updateCart(); // Update the cart display
        document.getElementById("productQuantity").value = 1; // Reset the quantity input
        localStorage.setItem('cart', JSON.stringify(shoppingCart.getItems())); // Save cart to
local storage
    }
}
```

```javascript
// Function to update the cart display
function updateCart() {
    const cartContainer = document.getElementById("cartContainer");
    cartContainer.innerHTML = ''; // Clear the cart container
    shoppingCart.getItems().forEach(cartItem => {
        const cartElement = document.createElement("div");
        cartElement.className = 'cart-item'; // Add cart-item class
        cartElement.innerHTML = `
            <span>${cartItem.product.name} - $${cartItem.product.price.toFixed(2)} x ${cartItem.quantity}</span>
            <input type="number" value="${cartItem.quantity}" min="1" onchange="updateCartItem(${cartItem.product.id}, this.value)">
            <button class="btn btn-danger" onclick="removeCartItem(${cartItem.product.id})">Remove</button>
            `;
        cartContainer.appendChild(cartElement); // Add the cart item to the container
    });
    document.getElementById("totalPrice").textContent = `Total Price: $${shoppingCart.calculateTotal().toFixed(2)}`; // Update total price
}


// Function to update the quantity of a cart item
function updateCartItem(productId, quantity) {
    shoppingCart.updateQuantity(productId, parseInt(quantity)); // Update quantity in the cart
    updateCart(); // Update the cart display
    localStorage.setItem('cart', JSON.stringify(shoppingCart.getItems())); // Save cart to local storage
}


// Function to remove a cart item
```

```javascript
function removeCartItem(productId) {
    shoppingCart.removeItem(productId); // Remove item from the cart
    updateCart(); // Update the cart display
    localStorage.setItem('cart', JSON.stringify(shoppingCart.getItems())); // Save cart to
local storage
}


// Event listener for adding an item to the cart
document.getElementById("addToCartBtn").addEventListener("click",
handleAddToCart);


// Initialize the page on load
document.addEventListener("DOMContentLoaded", () => {
    const savedCartItems = JSON.parse(localStorage.getItem('cart')); // Load cart items
from local storage
    if (savedCartItems) {
        savedCartItems.forEach(cartItemData => {
            const product = products.find(product => product.id ===
cartItemData.product.id); // Find product by ID
            if (product) {
                const cartItem = new CartItem(product, cartItemData.quantity); // Create a cart
item
                shoppingCart.addItem(cartItem)
                    shoppingCart.addItem(cartItem); // Add the cart item to the shopping cart
            }
        });
        updateCart(); // Update the cart display with the loaded items
    }
    updateProductSelection(); // Update the product selection dropdown
});
```

Exercise 4.4

Html File :

```html
<!DOCTYPE html>
<html lang="en">
<head>
  <meta charset="UTF-8">
  <meta name="viewport" content="width=device-width, initial-scale=1.0">
  <title>Messaging System</title>
  <style>
    body {
      font-family: Arial, sans-serif;
      background-color: #f0f0f0;
      margin: 0;
      padding: 0;
      display: flex;
      justify-content: center;
      align-items: flex-start;
      padding-top: 50px;
    }

    .container {
      display: flex;
      gap: 20px;
    }

    .inbox, .form-container, .login-container {
      background-color: #fff;
      border-radius: 8px;
      box-shadow: 0 0 10px rgba(0, 0, 0, 0.1);
      padding: 20px;
      width: 400px;
    }
```

```css
.inbox h1, .form-container h1, .login-container h1 {
    text-align: center;
    margin-bottom: 20px;
    color: #333;
}

.welcome-message {
    text-align: center;
    margin-bottom: 20px;
    color: #333;
    font-size: 1.2em;
}

.message-list {
    margin-bottom: 20px;
}

.message {
    border-bottom: 1px solid #eee;
    padding: 10px 0;
}

    .message:last-child {
        border-bottom: none;
    }

    .message .details {
        display: flex;
        justify-content: space-between;
        margin-bottom: 5px;
    }
```

```css
.message .details .sender,
.message .details .recipient,
.message .details .timestamp {
    font-size: 0.9em;
    color: #777;
}

.message .content {
    font-size: 1em;
    color: #333;
}

.form-group {
    margin-bottom: 15px;
}

.form-group label {
    display: block;
    margin-bottom: 5px;
}

.form-group input, .form-group textarea {
    width: 100%;
    padding: 8px;
    box-sizing: border-box;
    border: 1px solid #ccc;
    border-radius: 4px;
}

.form-group textarea {
    resize: vertical;
```

```
        }

    button {
        display: block;
        width: 100%;
        padding: 10px;
        background-color: #007bff;
        color: white;
        border: none;
        border-radius: 4px;
        cursor: pointer;
    }

    button:hover {
        background-color: #0056b3;
    }
    </style>
</head>
<body>
    <div id="auth-container" class="login-container">
        <h1>Login</h1>
        <div class="form-group">
            <label for="username">Username</label>
            <input type="text" id="username" placeholder="Enter your username">
        </div>
        <div class="form-group">
            <label for="password">Password</label>
            <input type="password" id="password" placeholder="Enter your password">
        </div>
        <button onclick="login()">Login</button>
    </div>
```

```html
<div id="main-container" class="container" style="display: none;">
  <div class="inbox">
    <h1>User Inbox</h1>
    <div id="welcomeMessage" class="welcome-message"></div>
    <div>
      <h2>Received Messages</h2>
      <div id="receivedMessageList" class="message-list"></div>
    </div>
    <div>
      <h2>Sent Messages</h2>
      <div id="sentMessageList" class="message-list"></div>
    </div>
  </div>
  <div class="form-container">
    <h1>Send Message</h1>
    <div class="form-group">
      <label for="recipient">Recipient</label>
      <input type="text" id="recipient" placeholder="Enter recipient's name">
    </div>
    <div class="form-group">
      <label for="content">Message</label>
      <textarea id="content" rows="4" placeholder="Enter your message"></textarea>
    </div>
    <button onclick="sendMessage()">Send Message</button>
  </div>
</div>

<script src="MessagingSystem.js" > </script>
</body>
</html>
```

JavaScript File (MessagingSystem.js):

```javascript
// Define the Message class
```

```javascript
class Message {
    constructor(sender, recipient, content, timestamp = new Date()) {
        this.sender = sender;
        this.recipient = recipient;
        this.content = content;
        this.timestamp = timestamp;
    }
}


// Define the UserInbox class
class UserInbox {
    constructor() {
        // Load messages from localStorage or initialize an empty array
        this.messages = JSON.parse(localStorage.getItem('messages')) || [];
    }


    // Method to send a message and save it to localStorage
    sendMessage(sender, recipient, content) {
        const message = new Message(sender, recipient, content);
        this.messages.push(message);
        localStorage.setItem('messages', JSON.stringify(this.messages));
    }


    // Method to get received and sent messages for a specific user
    getMessagesForUser(user) {
        return {
            received: this.messages.filter(msg => msg.recipient === user),
            sent: this.messages.filter(msg => msg.sender === user)
        };
    }
}
```

```javascript
// Create an instance of UserInbox
const inbox = new UserInbox();
let currentUser = null;

// Function to handle user login
function login() {
    const username = document.getElementById('username').value;
    const password = document.getElementById('password').value;
    const users = {
        sara: 'pass1',
        jan: 'pass2',
        dina: 'pass3'
    };

    // Check if the username and password match any user
    if (users[username] && users[username] === password) {
        currentUser = username;
        // Hide the login form and show the main container
        document.getElementById('auth-container').style.display = 'none';
        document.getElementById('main-container').style.display = 'flex';
        // Display a welcome message
        document.getElementById('welcomeMessage').innerText = `Welcome,
${currentUser}!`;
        // Display messages for the logged-in user
        displayMessages(inbox.getMessagesForUser(currentUser));
    } else {
        alert('Invalid username or password');
    }
}

// Function to display messages in the HTML
function displayMessages(messages) {
```

```javascript
const receivedMessageList = document.getElementById('receivedMessageList');
const sentMessageList = document.getElementById('sentMessageList');
receivedMessageList.innerHTML = '';
sentMessageList.innerHTML = '';

// Display received messages
messages.received.forEach(msg => {
    const messageDiv = document.createElement('div');
    messageDiv.className = 'message';

    const detailsDiv = document.createElement('div');
    detailsDiv.className = 'details';

    const senderSpan = document.createElement('span');
    senderSpan.className = 'sender';
    senderSpan.innerText = `From: ${msg.sender}`;

    const timestampSpan = document.createElement('span');
    timestampSpan.className = 'timestamp';
    timestampSpan.innerText = `Sent: ${new Date(msg.timestamp).toLocaleString()}`;

    detailsDiv.appendChild(senderSpan);
    detailsDiv.appendChild(timestampSpan);

    const contentDiv = document.createElement('div');
    contentDiv.className = 'content';
    contentDiv.innerText = msg.content;

    messageDiv.appendChild(detailsDiv);
    messageDiv.appendChild(contentDiv);

    receivedMessageList.appendChild(messageDiv);
```

```javascript
    });

    // Display sent messages
    messages.sent.forEach(msg => {
        const messageDiv = document.createElement('div');
        messageDiv.className = 'message';

        const detailsDiv = document.createElement('div');
        detailsDiv.className = 'details';

        const recipientSpan = document.createElement('span');
        recipientSpan.className = 'recipient';
        recipientSpan.innerText = `To: ${msg.recipient}`;

        const timestampSpan = document.createElement('span');
        timestampSpan.className = 'timestamp';
        timestampSpan.innerText = `Sent: ${new Date(msg.timestamp).toLocaleString()}`;

        detailsDiv.appendChild(recipientSpan);
        detailsDiv.appendChild(timestampSpan);

        const contentDiv = document.createElement('div');
        contentDiv.className = 'content';
        contentDiv.innerText = msg.content;

        messageDiv.appendChild(detailsDiv);
        messageDiv.appendChild(contentDiv);

        sentMessageList.appendChild(messageDiv);
    });
}
```

```javascript
// Function to handle sending messages
function sendMessage() {
    const recipient = document.getElementById('recipient').value;
    const content = document.getElementById('content').value;

    // Check if all fields are filled
    if (currentUser && recipient && content) {
        // Send the message using the inbox instance
        inbox.sendMessage(currentUser, recipient, content);
        // Clear the input fields
        document.getElementById('recipient').value = '';
        document.getElementById('content').value = '';
        // Refresh the displayed messages
        displayMessages(inbox.getMessagesForUser(currentUser));
    } else {
        alert('Please fill out all fields');
    }
}
```